KV-677-360

In loving memory
of
Kathleen McCauley Bamberger

Chingford O.A.

the god
of
the
group

*the influence
of being-in-a-group
on doing
theology*

GEORGE McCAULEY, S.J.

Argus Communications

Niles, Illinois

FIRST EDITION

© Copyright Argus Communications 1975

All rights reserved. No portion of this book may be reproduced, stored in a retrieval system, or transmitted in any form by any means—electronic, mechanical, photocopying, recording or otherwise—without prior permission of the copyright owner.

Printed in the United States of America.

ARGUS COMMUNICATIONS
7440 Natchez Avenue
Niles, Illinois 60648

International Standard Book Number 0-913592-63-3
Library of Congress Number 95-34903

1 2 3 4 5 6 7 8 9 0

contents

I

Laying
the
groundwork

If we gathered together the conversations people have had concerning the gods, the resulting flood of words, images, theories and systems would threaten to overwhelm us. This immense store of religious language varies greatly in style and talent. Some religious language is underprivileged, even inarticulate. Some is well-connected with intellectual movements. Enigma and paradox are found alongside rational argument. Often sage nodding accompanies religious talk, but the listener remains puzzled. Language about the gods can bore as well as uplift. It can be terribly misleading.

If we consider this or that specific religious tradition—and we will be speaking out of a Roman Catholic tradition in this book—the picture of religious language remains quite human. Far from being spoken from on high, religious language makes a humble entrance into the world. It is born, struggling for breath, at a point in time, in a definite place. It is baptized into a community, if it is not to remain in some cultural limbo. It may be confirmed by a powerful tradition and mature with age. It enters into honest union with other languages, religious or secular, and from this union new ways of expressing religious beliefs come forth. It is sometimes wrongheaded and proud. Celebrated for a time, soon much of it becomes a dead letter. In short, religious language comes from people and follows their fate.

It is a commonplace that people act one way in groups and another way when they are not in groups. It would seem to follow that religious language, as the product of people, will reflect the truth of the commonplace, and that God will get talked about as he does because of what is going on in the group that is doing the talking.

God is always pictured in human language. If this language picks up any special nuance or configuration because it comes from people acting in a group rather than individually, we may ask whether "the God of the group" differs measurably from God as individuals describe him. This is the basic kind of question we will be exploring.

There are many groups in which religious matters are discussed: theology classes, counselling sessions, preaching situations, bible study groups, official doctrinal synods of a Church, and so on. The people in these groups are all individuals of varied talents and educational levels. But they are also acting in a group. Is everything said by them the clear, objective and frankly religious kind of talk it seems to be? Or are things said that reflect not so much their religious thinking as their being-in-a-group, subject to the life of the group, its patterns and laws?

But what is meant by this "being-in-a-group"? It often comes as a surprise to people to realize to what extent patterns of group-behavior have been analyzed and studied. Yet there are whole sciences dedicated to the study of such behavior.[1] There are highly developed methods for the observation of people in groups. Great concern is had for the legitimacy, validity and implications of these methods. But their practitioners are all convinced that such study tells us something important about human reality.

That group-behavior can be patterned, traced, predicted and categorized is a shocking realization for many people. This news is often resented because many of us consider ourselves to be competent observers of human behavior, or because having one's behavior observed and commented upon seems to be an intrusion or a criticism. Furthermore, many confuse the study of group-behavior with sensitivity sessions or "worse."

The application of what we can learn about group-behavior to groups dealing with religious matters is doubly offensive to those for whom religion is very much a private affair. Even if a social dimension to religion is admitted, many consider Church-life to be beyond the influence of something so secular as group-science. Then, too, there is a practical despair of finding "better" or "more suitable" religious language, since this seems to imply a criticism of well-established religious expressions. Finally, the very idea of a God of the group appears, at this early stage, so spectral, so indefinite, that an initial uneasiness with the thought is quite legitimate.

And yet, the question remains: Do group-behavior patterns exert an influence on religious language? To what extent? This question necessitates a brief explanation of some of these patterns of group-life. Let us look, then, at some findings of responsible group scientists concerning behavior in groups.

Dependency

In groups with a common task, some people tend to await leadership and competence from others. They assume a helpless, infantile stance. They seek the comfort of being carried along in the group's work. They exalt the qualities of others who are doing the task, attributing almost magical powers to them. Then they hang suspended between jealousy and adulation of such powers.

At issue is always the competence of others in comparison with oneself: "What are my resources for this kind of task? More importantly, what are my resources for cooperating with others in this task? At the border of other people, how do I present myself, my credentials and connections, my negotiating skills, my declaration of intent? Would it not be easier to put these complicated matters into someone else's hands?"

The reasons for such dependent behavior can vary: a sense of inferiority, being overimpressed by titles, a distaste for the task, sheer habits of passivity, a fear of what happens (or is thought to happen) to the leaders among us. Or people associate, mistakenly or not, others' age, sex, demeanor or language with greater competence than their own.

Fight-flight

Manifestations of aggressive behavior in a group may be overt or subtle. We are familiar with the more obvious ones: shouting, insult, baiting, curtness, gross ignoring, and so forth. The ones which concern us here are those which appear when competition arises over the relative competence of those present for the task. Subtler forms of violence may then occur. This or that member may be given the silent treatment, others allowed to make fools of themselves, people pitted against each other by misquoting or by the use of explosive words in concealed contexts. Needless to say, the progress of the task is hampered while the group is in the midst of a melee, however controlled things appear on the surface.

As varied as the forms of fighting are, the ways in which people run from the task are no less so. When basic emotions concerning one's own competence are involved, or when others are shining their competence in one's eyes, it is understandable that people try to recoup their sense of self-esteem as best they can. Often this is through some kind of strategic flight, manifested in lethargy, hearing-difficulties, the vigorous pursuit of activities other than the one at hand, and physical or mental departures of one kind or another. Some of these phenomena are neutral in themselves; they can be responsibly productive or not. For example, silence can be a prudent expedient when other business is being done which must run its course before the task may reasonably be resumed. It is only when people run from the task by their silence that it takes on the negative significance that is described here.

Pairing

A third basic pattern of behavior may be discerned in groups. It is called pairing. This term attempts to describe a kind of behavior which aims at maintaining the existence of the group at all costs (even at the cost of not doing its common task). A pair of members, or successive and alternating pairs, engage in concentrated, ostensibly productive, and usually amicable dialogue or interrelating. This union appears to give hope to the others that something will be forthcoming in the group that will render its existence meaningful and fruitful. The image is frankly reproductive, but it is an image. It does not necessarily indicate forms of flirting or sexual attraction in the group. One writer describes how, when pairing is occuring, others in the group are passively hoping that the pair has gotten together to "save" the group. It will supposedly do this by bringing forth a new topic, a suggestion, or perhaps even a new leader who will justify the continued existence of the group:

> The group, through the pair, is living in the hope of the creation of a new leader, a new thought, or something which will bring about a new life, will solve the old problems and bring Utopia or heaven, or something of the sort. As in the history of the world if a new leader or Messiah is actually produced, he will of course shortly be rejected. In order to maintain hope, he must be unborn. [2]

Hence the rosy, unproductive period of pairing may continue in the group, giving it the dubious hope that all is well, when in fact it may have to go through much more suffering if it is to do its task.

Group-agency

It is important to note that the foregoing modes of behavior are to be attributed to the group as such and not to individuals in it. [3] The whole group has responsibility for the movements within it that advance or hinder the task. In other words, the members of the group are not merely spectators of each other's behavior; they are also instigators, victims, seducers and seduced.

Nowhere does this appear more vividly than when the group as a whole gets individuals in it to work out its own fears, or to represent some stage of advance that it is struggling through at a given moment. Making someone a scapegoat for the group's failure or a guinea pig are the most obvious examples. Scientific observers note that a group at times will avoid handling painful emotional problems of its own by attributing them exclusively to individuals within it or by pressuring individuals to give isolated expression to them. Thus it unconsciously diverts the focus of concern and resentment from itself. The group expresses its violence by drawing one of its members to violence. Or it transposes its own baser sexual urgings onto a member who becomes the sexy one of the group. Or it denies its own craving for unrestrained power by attributing that power excessively to one leader or suitable repository in the group. The group picks on someone to be the carrier of its own craziness, in-articulateness, hopelessness before the common task, its own resent-ment or fantasy concerning leadership, and so forth.

But not only are the group's negative feelings thus "split off" onto some particular member. The best resources of the group, its creativity, its imagination, its sensitivity, its determination to work, its sheer raw talent—all of which cause anxiety until their utilization is made possible by recognition and authorization—these too, are de-posited temporarily with one or another member of the group, and that member is forced to experiment for the others with their acceptability.

The selection of this or that particular member for such duties as described above usually takes the easiest possible route, namely, stereotyping (the professional type, the pious one, the milquetoast, the rugged individualist). People are given those roles that they are expected to have, whether this procedure is helpful to the common task or not. And God help the person who refuses to live up to his or her stereotype.

Stereotyping is not without a subtle reasonableness which is connected to the whole question of competence for the task. People who do not themselves feel competent, or who are uncertain, do however feel that particular qualities go to make up competence: experience, preparation, training, knowhow, and so on. The ster-eotype is thought to possess these qualities *ex officio*. In gravitating toward the stereotype under stress circumstances, the group is saying that "competence" is called for even for its digressions from the task.

Shadow-groups

Maurice Nedoncelle says that every individual walks around with an invisible entourage made up of many "selves."[4] We see ourselves as *many* people, according as we focus on this or that aspect of our personality, this or that stage of our resolve. Memory stores up images of ourselves from long ago. Each separate plan for the future involves an image of myself carrying it out. The entourage is the sum total of all these self-images. It is a friendly crowd or a rowdy one, confusing or easily accepted, depending on how we have integrated ourselves.

Something like this is true of groups. The individual in one group is tied by invisible bonds to other groups of which he is also a member. He brings this relationship with those other groups into the group he is presently a part of, creating there a shadow-effect from the outside groups. Not that those other groups—for example, the family or former associates—are insubstantial in themselves. But their business is not the business of the group he is *presently* engaged in. In this sense, measured against what the present group is trying to do they are called shadow-groups.[5]

Sometimes it can happen that many members of a group may share the same shadow-group. This creates the problem of discerning when the members of a group are truly acting as members of that group and when they are secretly engaged in the business of the shadow-group to which they all belong. All the workings and processes of a group—task definition, fighting, pairing, authorization, emotional transactions, dependencies, leadership, and so forth —have to be looked at, to see if they are the workings and processes of this group here and now, or whether they are being imported as baggage from the shadow-groups. In this study, for example, the members of a group that is supposedly working on theological language all belong to and share at least one shadow-group, the Roman Catholic Church. We will have to examine, then, how imports from that shadow-group influence the theologizing going on in the groups presented later in this book.

General remarks

Patterns of group behavior can be considered as they touch an *individual's* performance; or in relationship to the group as such. In the latter case, the important thing is not *that* dependency is going on, nor *that* it is going on in this individual, but rather what it is doing to the group's task performance. Fighting, scapegoating, and so on, are not being observed for their own sake, nor for the sake of any individual's improvement, but in explicit connection with how a group is working as a group toward a common goal. This is certainly the way we will be considering them. Our aim is to learn about the effect on the task of all the interrelated instances of dependency, fighting, and so on that occur. Too much attention to individual performance in these circumstances can even be harmful: If I am too interested, for example, in discovering how *I* might perform and figure in a symphony orchestra, I risk missing a great deal of what is going on in orchestras *as such*.

Another caution that is pertinent here is that we should not moralize about the patterns of group-behavior we have described. We should not conceive of them as planned, fully-free, and coldly responsible stratagems of the people involved. They are being considered rather as *functions* of a highly complex, diversely motivated and relatively unconscious group process. It is true that the group as such seems to have a built-in hunger for integrity in its task-performance. It also experiences great guilt when it engages in behavior that thwarts its cooperative success. The problem with many groups is that they have no structural mechanism for "forgiving" themselves. But, while the language of morality may find some analogous application to group-behavior, it is disastrous to the learning process to hear and see everything in terms of personal good or evil. On the other hand, we do not mean to imply that the patterns of group-behavior are so inevitable and dominant that we cannot overcome unfruitful behavior patterns, or integrate them constructively into the common task.

The patterns of group-behavior described earlier do not stand out as neatly compartmentalized segments of the group's life. In groups agenda are replaced, chain-reactions disrupt the configurations of the moment before, positions taken are soon abandoned, work done is dismantled, issues are raised like banners silently unfurled.

THE METHOD EMPLOYED IN THIS STUDY

These various group-phenomena also appear when groups have as their task talking about religion. To study their impact on what gets said theologically, a method was devised which serves as the basis for this study.

Volunteer group members were first recruited. They usually consisted of experienced religious educators or ministers engaged in masters' level programs. The groups consisted of about ten members each.[6]

These groups were then introduced to the overall theme and common task of the sessions, namely, to study the relationship between their group-behavior and their theologizing. They were not pre-instructed on the patterns of group-life which they would probably experience, but were exhorted in a general way to be aware of their group interaction as they proceded theologically, and to study the relationships between the two.

They were also given a specific theological task to do. These specific tasks consisted of simulated sacramental situations, in which there was always a common responsibility imposed on the group to explain to someone in their midst one or other of the sacraments. For example, the group's task might be phrased as follows:

> Our overall task is to study how our being in a group
> influences what eventually gets said about God,
> Jesus, sacraments, or, especially in this case,
> the sacrament of baptism.
> To this end the group is to baptize
> one of its members, with the proviso that it first
> shares the responsibility of explaining
> to the candidate what is thereby involved.

One reason why the sacraments were chosen as the theological issues for the groups to discuss is that the sacraments are an area of theology with which the author was familiar, and which he actually taught a great deal.[7] These teaching situations provided the opportunity for occasional group events. More importantly, sacraments are normally conducted in group settings in the life of the Church, and therefore lend themselves to this kind of inquiry.

The sessions lasted for about one-and-one-half hours, followed by a half-hour review of what took place. Where there were more people present than the usual ten in the working group, the others formed a corona of observers. This explains several references in the group-events described below to persons present who are not in the smaller, working group. The observers were provided with a list of things to look for as they observed the working group.[8] The working group received only a written copy of the task.

The author served as facilitator to the group's work. He made comments where there was an opportunity for the group to learn something about how its group-life might be influencing its theological progress. His interventions were always in the form of statements about the group as a group, not about individuals. He did not discuss these comments with the group, or respond to questions. The reasons for this aloofness were partly to let him concentrate on the overall task of the group, and partly as a symbol of his desire to direct the group to *its own* responsibility.

* * * * *

Some further comments on the method are in order. They are intended to prepare the reader more fully for the chapters that follow. They anticipate questions, set boundaries to expectations, provide the necessary nuances and map out landmarks or details to look for along the way. Some people are impatient with such preliminaries. They want to get under way, especially since many of the introductory points will make better sense after the individual group sessions have been studied. Such readers might skip, then, to the following chapters. To the rest these additional considerations are offered.

I. *The work set for the group is complicated.* First, the group must keep alert to its own group-life, to the issues and rhythms of group-behavior through which it is passing. Much of the group's energies is in fact riveted on its being-in-a-group, to the neglect of the theological task. Energy spent in this way is time-consuming and exhausting. The method is so devised that it galvanizes the group's awareness to aspects of its own performance such as personal responsibility, trust, authority, individual differences, competence, pluralism, and so on. Attention to these occupy a large part of the group's effort.

Second, the group has theological work to do. This work is not restricted to the sacraments, for attitudes and views about God and Jesus are implied in or raised by the sacraments. Very sensitive and trying implications are therefore involved. Third, the group has as its overall purpose to study the relationship between its own workings and the performance of its task. In short, the group has a lot to do.

So we have to ask whether or not it has so much to do, that it cannot be expected to do anything well. Does the method offer sufficient time or sufficient leisure to allow the group to show its authentic self, its true behavior and its real capacities?

Also, with the time-limits, with the techniques of the facilitator, with the simulation of sacramental situations, the method has a built-in artificiality about it. How can such a procedure show us anything?

The reader will have to judge about that from the chapters that follow. But several points can be considered here: the group members in question were all fairly experienced religious educators, for whom the topic of sacraments was hardly new. Furthermore, the dynamics of group-life are not something mysterious and beyond everyone's reach. They are, and always were, at work in our real life situations, and we are often marginally aware of them as we try to do specific tasks in life. We cannot suppose that, in focusing more attention on them than we normally do, we are entering into a totally new area. Finally, we might have thought that the pressure and artificiality of the group sessions would surface *less* information about how group-life influences theologizing. But in fact the pressurized atmosphere seems to accelerate what we learn.

II. *More problematic is the role of the facilitator.* He must be alert to the group-life. His job too is to study how the *process* of that group-life influences the *content* of the theology being expressed by the

9

group. He must help the group both to see the process they are involved in and to see where they have arrived theologically at any given point. His general knowledge might tell him that groups are *generally* agitated by competition, fear, prejudice, coalitions, resentments, guilt, excursions, stolid pursuit of the task at the price of others' feelings, solo flights of creativity or of pique. But how these various movements are affecting a *specific* group here and now, and how this is influencing their specific theological work—this is the facilitator's arduous concern.

There are many ways to go wrong. The facilitator might concentrate too much on the group-life; he might shy away from aspects of the group process that could tax his talents; or he might concentrate too much on the theological dimension with which he is more comfortable and hence more easily distracted; he might be anxious to impose his vision of the theological content of sacraments on the group; he has to discern whether the group's theological talk is to be taken at face value (as serious theologizing) or whether it is a covert way by which the group is doing "other business" related to its group-life; in doubtful situations, he sometimes has to use remarks about theological *content* in order to get the group to look at the group *process,* and vice-versa.

While the author is not an expert in the study of group-behavior, he hoped that his familiarity with group-behavior analysis was sufficient to inaugurate the experiment reported in this book. The influence of group-life on theology is practically virgin territory. So any attempt to wed the two areas is going to be tentative, an initial, groping exploration. We have to hope that others will follow in the paths explored here, and improve upon the techniques and methods used.

III. *The theology of sacraments with which the facilitator is working also figures importantly in the method which is used.* Just as he inevitably "reads" the group according to assumptions he has about group processes, so too he judges whether and where theological work is going on in the group according to his assumptions about theology. Hence, it is necessary to set forth those assumptions.

At the end of this chapter, his overall view of sacrament as such will be found. In the *first section* of subsequent chapters (II-VII) his theological presuppositions concerning the individual sacrament in question are set forth. These presuppositions have *already* been influenced by the author's experimentation over several years with groups doing theology. Because theology is not static, when old thoughts are brought into contact with new materials or new sciences, an immediate cross-fertilization takes place. We must candidly wonder where our new theological thoughts began and how we should trace their advance. This is true of the accounts of theological presuppositions found in each chapter. Each already expresses something of what can be learned from a group-perspective.

The *second section* of each chapter contains the narration of the group event. There our attention is directed to how the group as a group arrives at its theology. A *third section* in each chapter explores the theological implications that could be drawn from the group's experience to advance the understanding provided in the first section.

A more obvious worry is that, because of his theological presuppositions, the facilitator will be proving through the groups what he wanted to prove anyway. How does the facilitator avoid reading things into the group-life, simply in order to explain why the group is not theologizing as he thinks it should? By his interventions, his supposed competence, his manner and method, the facilitator seems to be in an unassailable position, but one in which the dangers of subjectivity are great. There is no easy way out of this dilemma. It is one that faces even the most "objective" scientists, historians, artists or journalists. The group members have a responsibility to think and act for themselves. The facilitator should not prevent them from defending any theological position they wish to defend. He tries to honor this in his observation of the groups. If they fail to take a different theological direction, this in itself is instructive for our general theme. Other than that, we can do no more than look critically at *what happens* in the groups, and to compare that with the theology offered.

IV. *The reader will get the impression that some of the group-sessions were largely negative experiences, complicated beyond imagining.* Even the language we have used thus far to describe patterns of group-life is turbulent and emotional. It depicts what might seem a contorted series of maneuvers. It challenges our general impression that groups are mostly calm, controlled, business-as-usual affairs, or, at worst, dull and boring. The picture of the groups analyzed in this book may not seem flattering. Much of this impression is due to the brevity of the group sessions. They were relatively short, and they represent the most intense part of the ordinary struggle of a group as it tries to get off the ground. It takes time for the creativity and leadership of any group to emerge.

On the other hand, most real-life religious education sessions *are* short. Even if they were not, we should never expect a group so to transcend the kinds of behavior described here that it would ever totally be free of them. For the group-life must constantly be brought into line with the group's task, not only to ward off negative elements, but to bring to bear the greatest talent and creativity on the task. What we will be looking for are certain theological *directions* that the group takes when it is advancing in its group-life. What does it then do to further explanation? Where does it go for its language, for illustration, for developing its thought? We hope to show that, despite the time limits, certain directions emerge which more positively show the group's potential for theology and not merely its difficulties with it. These directions we will explore in the last chapter.

V . *We have used a variety of ways of transcribing the group sessions*. The full script is not given because it makes such rambling reading. Instead, a narrative of the sessions is usually offered. The sequence of the narrative is true to the actual session that took place, and exact quotations are preserved and worked into the narrative. In one case (the ordination group), the group session is described in terms of the issues raised during it, although even there the original sequence is mostly preserved. As we will see, the sessions involve a great deal of back-and-forth and overlapping between the theological work of the group and the group's preoccupation with issues of its inner-life. Names used are fictitious.

BACKGROUND ON SACRAMENTAL THEOLOGY

We should now sketch the general approach to sacraments that will be operative throughout this book. The history of sacramental theology has followed several trends.

I. Sacramental theology had always considered sacraments as *sacred signs or symbols*. This traditional stance received new impetus during the past hundred years, when developments in the history of religions, in comparative religion and in the philosophy of symbols created an intellectual atmosphere in which the Christian, with his wealth of religious symbols, could feel especially at home. The emphasis in much of that literature was on the specific quality of symbols. Like signs, symbols pointed a person elsewhere. They referred him to something beyond themselves and beyond the subject who used them. Signs had a more restricted power to refer, and a more limited significance. The sign indicated, for example, where the balcony was situated, and that was the end of the matter. If one wanted to find another balcony elsewhere, he had to find another sign. Signs told the person who could ''read sign'' that a party of four had passed along the route, and so on. Not only was the objective reference of signs narrow, but the concomitant subjective state of the person was thought to be little affected. Signs gave rise to little emotional involvement.

Symbols, on the other hand, were richly broad in their objective reference, and they engaged the subject who used them at many interior levels. Water, fire, earth, swastikas, sacred trees and even, under certain circumstances, balconies—these symbols contained, it was thought, a range of power. They threatened, enticed, promised, summoned, hinted, urged, intimated strangely. They were carriers of truth that transcended themselves, of beauty that led the eye past themselves to mysterious horizons. In symbols, the integration or upheaval of the self was often at stake. The sacramental symbols were inserted into this range of cosmic symbols, and the similarity of Christian symbolism with the world's religious symbols was highlighted.[9]

II. A second trend of *sacramental theology* stressed the difference between Christian symbols and the cosmic symbols of the world religions. In this trend it was pointed out that the great symbols of the Judeo-Christian tradition were always tied to some historical reference. What was important, for example, was not water as symbol but *the* waters that figured in the history of salvation, which gave special nuance to the powerful innate symbolism of water itself. Thus, the waters of creation, the flood, the Red Sea, the Jordan, the water that flowed from Christ's side—all contributed to the understanding of water symbolisms for Christians. The cosmic symbols became incarnate in the privileged events surrounding one people, the people of Israel, and one person, Jesus of Nazareth. The energy spent on tracking down the biblical-historical nuance of the great cosmic symbols was great. The study of sacramental theology demanded the study of all the anointings, sacral meals, healings and lustrations in the Judeo-Christian tradition. This trend in sacramental theology was largely the fruit of developments in scriptural, patristic, and liturgical studies. Whatever systematic insight and intelligibility there was in this sacramental theology was determined by what those fields of study could provide.[10]

III. At the level of the average Catholic adult's life, it is doubtful that these trends made much of an impact. For many, sacraments remained neither signs nor symbols but rather *signals*. A signal is action-oriented. When it is given, someone begins to perform or something starts to happen. Many Christians effectively looked upon the sacraments as actions which, when performed correctly, signalled *God* to go into action and perform favorably in man's regard. Understood thus, the nature, content, style, history, humanity, or even the meaning of the signals themselves were of secondary importance.

The fact that they triggered God's involvement was primary. And God, after all, seems to have been the one who set up the signal-system in the first place. Much sweat went into the question of when the signal was properly confected; comparatively little attention was paid to the faith and dispositions of the recipients, not to mention of the ministers.

IV. Possibly in reaction to the rather demeaning view of sacraments just described, more recent theologies of sacraments have stressed the personal and prayerful aspect of sacraments. Through sacraments we are brought into God's presence, we encounter the mystery of God. The sacraments are signs of the risen Jesus' continuing presence to his Church, so that man's engagement with him is carried on in the life of the Church mainly through the sacraments. The "presence" and "encounter" here envisioned are at once real contact with God and at the same time movement toward ultimate eschatological union and solidarity with God in Christ. Sacraments are not only signs of the transcendent but also of the reign of God to come. They are a drawing of all to God, a way in which God gathers his community in preparation for its final encounter with himself, in which alone will people finally encounter and be truly present to each other.[11]

V. Several sacramental theologies underscored the *human impact* in sacraments. They emphasized the parallelism between the sacraments and key events or experiences that occur in human life (birth, death, marriage, guilt, etc.). This parallelism led some theologians to see sacraments as deliberately designed by God to enable us to pass through the important stages of human life. Sacraments would enable us to integrate these stages into our faith in Jesus, to go through them with God. The parallelism, then, was not accidental. "A sacrament is always the culminating point of an (secular) event set in motion in us by God." The continuity of sacraments with the aspirations of our humanity would include in particular the desire of people for community. This desire is pervasive. Even in the secular things we do, we search for a people-environment in which we can do them with a solidarity and reinforcement that only other people can provide. The sacraments, as actions of the community, would also provide this important human dimension of community.[12]

VI. Much sacramental theology was done in terms of an often profound scholastic analysis which centered on such questions as how sacraments are said to signify, how they give grace, what their ultimate intelligible structure and constitution are. The aim here was frankly *metaphysical,* and this kind of sacramental theology has suffered the same fortunes as metaphysics has in recent years.[13]

VII. Sacraments have also functioned as *insignia,* as the means of identifying where people are located on a socio-religious scale. Little has been written on this function of sacraments, but it might be more prevalent than we think. Thus, the Catholic would be characterized by his sacramental system. By it, his socio-religious identity would be measured, his allegiance known, his expectations predicted, his associations made more or less predictable, his success or failure charted in a recognizable way. By it, he is easily differentiated from members of other societies, who have either no sacraments or fewer. If he goes to the sacraments, he remains within an identifiable institutional structure, and thus finds a sense of belonging and cohesion with a mass of others. If he stays away from the sacraments, he reports that fact precisely as a crisis of identification with something that he is supposed to be in the public forum. His birth, his marriage, the birth of his children, his dying, all are part of a formal structure which regulates those events and gives them a social acceptance. This view of sacraments is lived rather than held. It attests to the force of the sacramental system in fixing the Catholic's moorings and in affording him those large landmarks whereby he can gauge the familiarity of his surroundings.

* * * * *

These trends in sacramental theology are not clear-cut and compartmentalized.[14] There are many points at which they complement each other, and even demand each other if they are to make sense. The scriptural emphasis, for example, limits our tendency to make anything out of sacraments that we wish. It saves us from ending up in the embarrassing position of so defining sacrament that our definition could cover anything from a sunset to a kiss, from a newly formed friendship to a picnic swim. The theology of presence and encounter is rich in the sense of transcendence and of prayer. It also, and rightfully, highlights the incompleteness of our present sacramental activity. But it can sink to the level of mystification if it does not try to explain how one sacramental encounter differs from another, how each presence is to be specifically conceived. It also could become simply a more sophisticated and benign version of the signal-approach to sacraments. The humanistic theology of sacraments is its best protection against these dangers because the God who is encountered according to that theology is candidly interested in specific issues which touch people. This theology, however, has

15

its own perversion, which occurs when sacraments are made a matter of human ingenuity and achievement to the extent that God's favor to us is lost sight of. The sociological interpretation of sacraments warns us that we might be using sacraments in the most extrinsic way, as insignia. But it also underscores more than any other approach the communitarian nature of sacraments, their force as programmatic statements of a community's deepest social beliefs.

A false understanding of the metaphysical theology of sacraments leads to a special problem in sacramental theology, the "matter-form" mentality. According to this mentality, the sacrament is supposedly made up of some material symbol (water, bread, wine, oil, or even imposed hands) and some verbal formulation. Both the cosmic symbolism approach and the scriptural approach to sacraments tended to get locked into this emphasis on material symbols. While sacraments involve material symbols, we have not exhausted the meaning of sacrament when we have traced the material symbols through world literature, scripture and tradition. A fuller appreciation of the sacramental action requires us to examine *what it is about that action* that calls for this or that material symbol, or this or that appropriate formulation. *What* are we trying to embody through our material symbols? *What* are we trying to put into words through our formulae?

* * * * *

In the theology operative in this book, sacraments are considered as activities which express specific, enduring values of the community, and ultimately of Jesus.[15] These activities are indeed signs, but in the sense that they are significant expressions of a valuing personality. A person takes a certain character, a signature, from his values. By the things he stands for, by his concerns and priorities over a period of time, he becomes—to borrow a beautiful expression that Leo the Great uses of sacraments—*conspicuous* for these things. In consequence of his full and true humanity, Jesus has his values. Being authentic values, they were first and foremost expressive of what he prized for his own self. They were not held by him solely for the potential edification they might afford others.

If we accept the hypothesis that sacraments convey, however residually, a picture of Jesus' values, then we are talking about: bringing people together in community, bringing about a mature level of involvement in that community's affairs, forgiving others, caring for the sick and dying, critically estimating what is to pass for love among men and women, doing things in the community with the appropriate organizational sophistication, and, finally, properly loving oneself and others in relation to the love that God has for us.

We have called the sacraments the residue of Jesus' values. This is not meant in any derogatory way. Jesus' institution of sacraments would consist basically in a communication by him of his values to others. This means that he would project his values into the arena of his followers with sufficient frequency, sufficient emphasis, sufficient definition and clarity, to indicate (symbolic in this sense) his own valuing personality. The important thing about those values was not how they were embodied or formulated through some material symbol or verbal expression, but their content as values. Hence, reading Scripture in a way that is tied to looking for traces of matter-and-form will yield only an impoverished view of sacraments. On the other hand, the hypothesis we are proposing would give a badly needed impetus to the attempt to uncover sacramental "references" in Scripture.

Often we are led to think that Jesus was interested in instituting little more than a series of ritual activities devoid of any exciting significance. The picture of the institutor of sacraments can be particularly devastating when we see some of the mechanistic, trivializing or hazy views of sacraments that people live with. On the other hand, we can be sympathetic with the process whereby sacraments become less than they could be when we reflect on how difficult it would be in a large community to keep such a stunning series of values alive.

Jesus' communication of his values to others follows the normal dynamics of human communication. That is, communications are heard, assimilated, translated, repeated, quoted, garbled, judged, measured, practiced or divided according to the capacity of the listeners, the clarity of the speaker, the rapport that has been established and the difficulty or ease of the content. If sacraments become empty rituals, we suggest that it is because that is all the traffic can bear in the Christian community. It is doubtful that such a judgment should come as a shock to anyone, including Jesus. The meaningfulness of sacraments is not something that happens automatically, simply because God's promise is associated with them. Rather, that meaningfulness must be fought for, established and re-established constantly.

Finally, this value approach to sacraments tries to preserve what is best in the approaches described earlier. The cosmic symbols remain, but they are tied even further into history in the person of Jesus and in his valuing. The salvation-history approach is honored, but caution is urged to be clear about one's presuppositions in any sacramental reading of Scripture. The signal approach to sacraments is retained only in the sense that the sacraments send *us* into action, into activities whose importance we learn from Jesus. Presence and encounter are kept, but we are encountering someone with specific things on his mind. The union with God that the sacraments achieve refreshes us at the same time as it reminds us that much work is to be done before the Kingdom comes. Sacraments deal with human activities, but not without passing through the prism of Jesus' followers. They provide the stuff of earnest and serious movements: a program of action, a powerful tradition, a hero and an oath sworn.[16]

II

The
baptism
group

I. BACKGROUND*

Jesus does not simply have a message. Rather, he assumes the role of
a rabbi within a community which he actively begins and with which
he is going to have ongoing contact. Given the emphasis in much
modern theology on Jesus as witness, or as prophet, and as a re-
vealer of the eschatological Kingdom, this fact of Jesus' formation
of a community can be lost sight of. And yet, it is that value of Jesus
that is the central presupposition of the sacrament of baptism. We
can make too much of the primitive community's supposed trans-
formation of Jesus-the-preacher into Christ-the-preached, and forget
that he was their organizer before he was preached about by them.[1]
They follow him; they go out on missions of various sorts and return
to him; they are indentified with him and attacked with him; they
celebrate with him and pray with him. From the outset he seems to
have had a sense of his formative role both in the community's
origin and its development. This can be said without entering into
the debate over whether Jesus intended to found a Church. Whatever
he intended to do, it was to be done in a somewhat organized and
communal way.

*See p. 10.

19

Whether the historical Jesus practiced baptism as a way of introducing his followers into his community is a complicated question which we need not enter into here. Certainly his followers used baptism as a sign of their cooperation with him in forming his kind of community. The New Testament writers assume that newcomers to the community are to be baptized. Interestingly enough, when they describe Jesus' own baptism by John, they place that event (whose exact historical position is hard to pin down due to the redactional work of the evangelists) quite close to Jesus' calling of the first disciples.[2] This serves to underline the tie-in between baptism and Jesus' interest in forming a community of like-minded followers.

In any case, we must not overdo the ritual aspect of baptism. Jesus' purpose in forming the community is *hardly* to insure the future of the baptismal *rite itself.* Rather, it is to organize those who, through whatever ritual initiation, enter on a new way of life in community. So when the New Testament speaks of certain effects of baptism, we may legitimately take these statements as an attempt to describe *the kind of community* into which Jesus wants to initiate his followers. Thus, we will gather New Testament observations on baptism to get a picture of what characterizes and distinguishes Jesus' community as a community, what it is engaged in, and what this means for the one who is to be baptized.

A. Accordingly, "baptism for the remission of sins" indicates that one is beginning in a community *dedicated to the mutual forgiveness of sins,* a community full of the assurance given by Jesus of the Father's forgiving love for it.[3] It is primarily the recipient's *subsequent* moral life that is envisaged in considering baptism as the remission of sin. As I Peter (3:21) puts it: "Baptism, which corresponds to (Noah's ark), now saves you also, not as the mere removing of physical stain, but as the craving of a conscience right with God."

B. "Baptism in the name of Jesus" indicates that the community considers itself under the protection of Jesus. His good name gives it respectability before God. He is the intercessor for it with the Father. Baptism in his name allows one to ask in his name. All this demonstrates the community's conviction about *his privileged status with the Father,* so that belief in this too will be a fixed mark of the community.[4]

C. By baptism the Spirit is bestowed.[5] Bultmann argues cogently that this usually signifies something about the community itself, namely, that it is a community *beyond sect,* and beyond that exclusivity that characterized Judaism.[6] This openness will be distinctive of the Christian community, in whose midst the gentiles will find a home. The follower of Jesus then finds himself in surprising company. In addition, the Spirit of Jesus has the role of opening up the community to a richly *diverse input* from its *individual members*. The unique talents and differences of those who join will have to be respected and developed. That uniformity which is the bane of all sects will have to be constantly challenged.

D. "Baptism into the body of Christ" carries with it similar connotations. In the thinking of Paul, there is to be an *organic interworking* of all in the community according to their *special capacities* and charisms.[7]

E. Finally, "baptism into the death and resurrection of Jesus" also serves as a description of the baptismal community.[8] It repeats the point made earlier (in B above) that Jesus' fidelity to his Father plays a key role in mediating the Father's favor of life to men. The Father is so impressed by Jesus' "death" that he raises Jesus to a new life and promises the same to everyone who is baptized. But there is no magic parallelism between a Christian's baptism and Jesus' death and resurrection, no arbitrary effectiveness assigned to the rite of baptism by which the Christian is joined to Jesus' fate.

The connection between baptism and that death-resurrection event is quite intelligible and meaningful. For it was not lost on the community which developed the death-resurrection language of baptism that Jesus died *for the way he lived*. His "death" is not an isolated act. It is the culmination of his life-style. It is what happens to him because of his stance, his values, his fidelity. So also in baptism, the thought is implied that the community is going to be *living* a certain way, a way that might get them killed as it got Jesus killed, but a way that, by God's favor, leads to resurrection as surely as Jesus' did. The "death" meant by Christian baptism is, then, an abandoning of former life-styles, in order to practice a life like Jesus'. As Jesus says, "Are you willing to be baptized with the baptism whereby I am baptized?"

* * * * *

So it is important to specify further what it was about Jesus' life that was to be preserved in the community's value structure and carried out in its life-style. The New Testament does this, as we have just seen, in the loosest terms. The subsequent ecclesial tradition, in its baptismal language, narrowed down even more what this com-

21

munity was specifically to stand for as a way of life. It spoke of baptism as "the gate of all the other sacraments." This was not the obvious commentary on some sacramental time-sequence that it seems to be. It implied that this community was to be the place where the other sacraments are to be practiced. These sacraments describe the interests and concerns of the baptismal community. This does not mean that the baptismal community later invented the other sacraments. It simply means that they articulated charity along lines they felt were first sketched out by Jesus.

Baptism itself is no more and no less than the entry into the kind of community we have been trying to picture from the foregoing New Testament references. This entry is the favor done us, but it is hard to focus on this simple truth. Nothing is sadder than people who are anxious (forget for a moment the unexpressed resentment) to have their child baptized "lest something terrible happen to it." There is little sense of baptism being a *beginning* in such an attitude, much less a sense of it being a beginning in community. Moreover, the kind of God presupposed by their anxiety is simply depressing. God's favor is made to depend upon a mechanical rite. The more obvious merits of baptism as an entry into a promising community are totally missing. Perhaps being in this community is not seen by them as a favor but as "a terrible thing happening." Perhaps they are even transferring to God what are really attitudes toward the community, so that the relationship with God is itself "terrible."

Certainly, we carry around with us attitudes about community and about our participation in it. These attitudes color our appreciation of baptism and our ability to talk about it. Some insist that community be nice. Some are concerned that penalties be known in advance. Most want to be sure that they can preserve their individuality in a community. Some look for a community they can disappear in. Some demand that all others in the community be firmly committed to its purposes, as though an intensity of community fervor is needed to carry them along. Others wish to know who is in charge, or what are the prestige positions, or how one advances to the fore. Still others despise titles or identifiable tasks. The usual discrimination on the basis of race, sex, age, seniority, economic, educational, or social class is also found. Some seek a guaranteed return on their input, especially in terms of the possibility of sharing interpersonally with others in the community; they abhor mere juxtaposition, placing friendship above all else. Others delve with great energy into the past of a community; they are greatly impressed by scandal, tradition, success, literary continuity, esteemed historical figures. Some emphasize uniforms, emblems, buttons and other insignia. Motivations for entering a community vary greatly. Some rush into community. Others go, following a friend, looking for danger, bored with where they are. Some are curious; some belligerent; many are cowed.

Now in all this, is it automatic that Jesus' kind of community corresponds to our spontaneous individual preferences? It is possible, but hardly likely. Where it does not, or where we do not know for sure whether it does, our attitudes toward beginning in that community are clouded. Sometimes this is true to such an extent that we do not even see what a simple, if important, thing is going on in baptism. Someone once suggested that we speak of baptism as bringing "one more warm body" into the Kingdom, so much did he feel that the matter of baptism was inflated in people's imaginations. We do tend to run together our doubts about the *nature* of Christ's community with the question of our *suitability* for it (as if God could not make us suitable). Then our doubt permeates the otherwise modest formality of entering that community. In the chapter on confirmation, we will discuss at greater length this matter of inflating beginnings. Suffice it to say here that our ability to describe the baptismal community, and therefore to talk about baptism, is subject to our general attitudes toward community and toward beginnings.

Forming community, as a value of Jesus, is, moreover, to be understood in an active rather than a passive sense. In terms of what is happening—a beginning in community—the recipient of the sacrament has a relatively simple role in the sacrament. But in terms of being on top of the event, realizing what the community is about, seeing how baptism relates to that, and so on, *the burden of the sacrament is on the baptizers*. It makes a great deal of difference whether we see the burden of Jesus' work placed on the recipient of the sacrament rather than on the doer of the sacrament. We have to ask ourselves whether Jesus gives us, in addition to the injunction to baptize, the resources to make that activity credible and persuasive to others.

The argument over infant baptism is revealing in this regard. Both the opponent and the supporter of infant baptism situate the recipient of the sacrament front row center. The supporter of infant baptism focuses so much on the recipient (the child must *be* baptized, in order to *be* saved), that the agency of the baptizers is little more than window dressing. The opponent of infant baptism pleads that the infant's freedom of choice is violated by it. In a roundabout way this plea does capture a sense of the community's agency in baptism, but only as potential violators of the child. However, the overriding assumption of the opponent is also that what happens in the recipient is the main burden of baptism. In both cases the agency of the baptizing community seems to be misplaced or ignored.

23

It is only with difficulty that we can set aside our fixation with the recipient of the sacrament. Yet, we know that anyone's fortune in the baptismal community depends upon many other factors besides simply entering it by receiving baptism. Even the question of whether we stay in that community depends on many other considerations: our fidelity, our coping, our luck, our enlightenment, developments in our personal conscience, our environment, and so on. No one could imagine that everyone who heard Jesus himself speak and failed to join his company did so in bad faith. No one could think that everyone who was joined to it and who subsequently left it did so at the cost of his own personal integrity. Being initiated into a community is hardly the same as putting one's hand to the plow, unless of course we think that every instance of being initiated implies the total personal commitment of the initiate. There is even the perplexing figure of the healer who worked in Jesus' name, but not in his baptismal company. These examples serve to show that neither all goodness nor all potential evil is worked out in the person of the recipient of the sacrament. The baptizers cannot escape so easily.

II. THE GROUP EVENT

Our overall task is to study how our being in a group
influences what eventually gets said about God,
Jesus, sacraments, or, especially in this case,
the sacrament of baptism.
To this end the group is to baptize
one of its members, with the proviso that it first
shares the responsibility of explaining
to the candidate what is thereby involved.

The group began by excusing itself for not being a community. This left the question hanging: how then could someone be baptized into it? Notwithstanding, Jane volunteered to be the candidate for baptism. She was asked what she saw in the group that would make her want to be baptized into it. *This question further reflected the group's sense of inferiority. This feeling will continue for some time. Jane's answer was flattering:* The group "looked like leaders;" "something seemed to be going on in it." The group allowed that, indeed, "prayer was going on in it," seemingly afraid at this point to claim more. Jane stated that she hoped, "to fit into a niche somewhere in it." *Did the members look to her, as they looked to the facilitator at this point, like statues?*

Jane was then asked what questions she might have about the community, what information or instruction she had previously received. Putting the burden in this way on Jane because of the

24

group's own diffidence was hardly fair, and Fred caught this. He suggested that the group instead should tell Jane how **it** saw **itself** as a community. His own contribution, however, succumbed to the same diffidence; he described the community as one which "often makes mistakes and needs help." Others tried to be more positive in their descriptions of the community: it brings Christ to others by the way it lives; it makes Christ's values real in the world; it makes Jesus' presence "more explicit" because of its eucharistic sign of Jesus' presence in its midst.

By these remarks the group was working toward a picture of the kind of community the candidate would be entering, although a certain anxiety to motivate Jane also was present. *This shifting between description and motivation occurred frequently.* It might explain why the group next gave a series of personal testimonies about what they as individuals had gained from their membership, what value and "reality" they found in the community. "That," they said, "was why they came and why they stayed." Jane responded that she too wished to be "real," and that it would take her a while to get to know the group. "After all," she said, "this is just a beginning." *No reaction.* She was reminded once more by the group that, "it was a struggling group," that it, "talked a lot about community without knowing what community was." All they knew was that the Church was not the same as the physical plant!

While the group was engaged, as it had been, in assessing its own reality, worth, performance, and happiness, the task was being made subordinate to these considerations. Very little description of baptism was being offered Jane, save a series of highly personal ones. So the facilitator asked the group, "whose baptism was it talking about." He was trying to get the group back on the track by opening up the more historical, objective question of what Jesus might have envisaged by baptism.

The facilitator's intervention seemed to add to the mood of diffidence in the group. Betty resumed the previous pessimistic train of thought, saying that the group, "was not a community, except at liturgy." Fred said that it was hard for the group to do anything else but talk of "its own experience," and, "in that connection," he thought the group should talk about Jesus' own baptism, how it was the beginning of his community, how that community possessed certain specific values, and so forth. *The latter remarks were obviously a reluctant restatement of things said by the facilitator in earlier lectures. The reluctance with which they were brought forth, together with the general mood of diffidence, seemed to indicate how troubled the group was to be dependent on someone else's knowledge. While this someone could be the facilitator, it could also be anyone in the room*. In fact, the point made by Fred had been made earlier by others in the room, but no one had responded to the persons making it at the time. That this lack of response was on the group's mind becomes apparent in what next developed.

The aspect of Jesus which struck the group in relation to baptism was his openness and lack of prejudice, in contrast to the group who had prejudices, "because of the family we grew up in." Jesus was concerned for others; he believed in the necessity and possibility of community; he wanted to be people's support. Jane, embarrassed perhaps by the group's struggle to show what all this had to do with baptism, asked the group whether people, "do these kinds of things in the parish?" Several members provided her with evidence: parishes had emergency consultation services; people were involved in religious education, helping the poor, prayer in the home, and so on. Betty added that more important than any of these examples was the fact that "we need one another," and that we can do what Jesus did only by sharing our labors. These themes of openness, support, concern, helping and sharing are not particularly trenchant descriptions of what goes on in the baptismal community. The group knows that there are many other communities in the world committed to these same values. *It seems, then, that these themes are also reflecting the preoccupations of the group at this point with its own inner struggle.*

The group returned to a consideration of Jesus' values, where it hoped to discover some content for a description of the Christian community. But again it was quickly distracted from this task. It went off instead onto two points. The first was that, whatever baptism enables us to do, it must be re-begun constantly by us. Thus, not only would Jane be baptized, but the group would be renewing its baptismal vows, too. By stressing this point, the group was giving the impression that there was no difference between an actual baptism and its future renewals. So the facilitator asked whether people were, in fact, "baptized all that often." If not, how was Jane's baptism different from the frequent renewals? Jane concurred with these misgivings about "daily baptisms." The group explained to her that, although the rite was over quickly, the commitment would go on. By this commitment, "we die every day in the hope of the resurrection," they said. Plato was cited to the effect that "we are all born to die." The group chose to describe baptism as a kind of death rather than as the beginning of a certain describable kind of life. While such language was certainly biblical, *in the context of the group-life it seemed rather to be conveying what the group was going through as it tried to interact with each other.* More importantly, a false theological alternative was being created:

26

either baptism was to be repeated daily or it was "just a rite." There was little sense of it being **just the beginning** of some **very important activities.** In addition, there was little clarity or detail about **what** one would be renewing or recommiting oneself to, except perhaps some vague cooperation with Jesus.

What fixed the group on this concern for future renewals was paradoxically its guilt about the past, its past failure to **choose** *its own baptism.* The group told Jane several times that it had chosen baptism. Since all the members were baptized as infants, this language was hardly candid. The facilitator pointed out the problem with it. Fred then admitted to Jane that she had a distinct advantage in freely approaching the sacrament. Apparently, the group was not sure whether its own baptism was an advantage, either because of the lack of choice involved, or because it could not explain very clearly what was to be chosen. That is why the choice connected with baptism grew to unbearable dimensions, requiring, "ongoing decisions about who Jesus is and who the community is, decisions based on the experience of the community."

Bravely, Joe tried to fight out of this impasse. He drew upon previous lectures to suggest that the remaining sacraments might serve to indicate what kind of community was on Jesus' mind. Baptism would then be the beginning of those meaningful activities implied in the other sacraments. This encouraged Harry to launch into a long description of the baptismal community, borrowing from Scripture, liturgical practice, and so on. Jane allowed that Harry's description was "really beautiful," but the rest of the group did not respond to Harry at all. This created the impression that *the group was once more allowing Jane to tell it what was or was not acceptable as a description of baptism.* The facilitator asked the group whether this indeed was what the group was doing at that moment.

This intervention evoked an angry response in the group, directed not at the facilitator but at Jane. "Jesus, after all, gave a **command** to be baptized," one member said, implying that such a command should be sufficient to make baptism "really beautiful." *As the group increasingly found itself faced with the necessity of reacting to one another in the task, they were not too happy at the prospect.* They pressed Jane to be finished, to be baptized. She responded by making a jumbled resume of the "great variety of thoughts" she had been presented with. The facilitator asked whether the group heard this resume as praise or condemnation, whereupon Fred told Jane *(the facilitator?)* that, although the group did not agree among themselves, it was doing the best it could. He jokingly suggested that Jane *(the facilitator?)* could join another group if she wanted.

The group fought against this tense atmosphere, in which threats of leaving, expelling, or finishing off were prevalent. The members adopted instead a very warm attitude toward each other. Being in the community, it was said, "makes us go," "makes us care for one another," "makes us feel good about ourselves and more peaceful." Jane was certainly anxious to keep the peace, and repeated her total readiness to be baptized. The group for its part reiterated its differences, its humanity, its fallible nature, its mistakes, and then asked Jane if she had "enough of an idea of the basics."

Picking up on one of the remarks made, the facilitator wondered out loud why "the traditional infallibility of the community had not been mentioned to the candidate?" The intervention was intended to get the group to see why it might be going through the very heart-to-heart phase it was in, full of great interpersonal reassurances but without much being said about baptism. When Harry suggested that someone "go get the water" to baptize the now all-too-willing and frightened Jane, the facilitator asked if the group was simply trying to end the pain. *This produced unchecked laughter.*

After this relief, the group tried once more to explain baptism to Jane, this time "getting at the basics." She would be entering a trinitarian community. She would receive a ritual sign of the cross on the forehead. The community was described as a royal priesthood, a consecrated nation—with foibles, of course. *The group still refused to study its own guilt, and the effect of this guilt on what got said to Jane,* so the facilitator challenged it again. He asked whether it was not perfectly normal and legitimate to introduce new members into an organization without immediately bringing up all the skeletons in that organization's closet. Why not put one's best foot forward? More than that, the facilitator asked the group how sincere it was about its admission of foibles. For, although the group *said* it had disagreements, foibles, problems, and so on, **up to that point no one had ever disagreed with what anyone else said.** Disagreement was admitted in theory, but never in practice.

This led to a long silence, broken eventually by this strange question from Jane, "Is the Catholic Church still one, holy, Catholic and apostolic?" *Jane was trying to save the group from its embarrassed silence* by returning to the task of describing the baptismal community in terms that could be shared by all. The group reacted limply to her question. Joe said that it was still very true, "despite our differences." Fred parodied the Gospel: "Wherever two or three are gathered together in disagreement, there I am in their midst." He also remarked that, at his baptism at least, he did not have to pass a test.

Conscious of the time-limit of the session, the group set about planning the baptism. God-parents, minister, and so on, were lined up. *Much of the language here was flight-language, the mention of distant places and situations indicating that the group wished it were somewhere else.* When it was suggested that the baptism take place at the offertory of a mass, the facilitator could not help but wonder whether reference was being made to an offering-victim. Another member suggested that the baptism could be done at a future Easter vigil, "that night of nights." Finally, when someone suggested that the group might as well confirm Jane, too, the session ended.

III. THEOLOGICAL IMPLICATIONS

We have seen the following factors at work in the group as it talked about baptism: First, there was a strong sense of guilt over the disagreements, confrontation and competition in the group. In every group there is potential violence, and violence does make people guilty. Moreover, for anything to be done by the group, relationships had to develop within it. These involve closeness, helping, trusting, and the like. But people feel guilty, too, about proximity of this sort.

Second, there was anger present in the group because, for one reason or another, people felt short-changed in their own baptism and resentful about assuming responsibility as baptizers. In the wider Church (their common shadow-group), they do not experience themselves as responsible agents of other people's baptisms. They have to "have it done," but they disassociate themselves from the doing of it. That role is said to be reserved to the (only) authorities in the Church, the hierarchical clergy, except in emergency cases when "even" (*sic*) a layman can perform the sacrament. At a later point in this book, we will discuss at length the extent to which this feeling of a lack of authority influences the work of our groups.

Third, guilt and anger intertwined when the group abandoned its responsibility of explaining baptism to the candidate and instead used the candidate to escape those moments when it was on the verge of confronting one another or coming too close to one another.

Fourth, the group got itself into a bind to the extent that it made the basis of its catechesis its own personal experience: what baptism has done **for me.** This tended to make the candidate dependent upon the rather private experiences of the group members. *Yet this private experience was the very thing the group refused to invade or have invaded in each other's case.* The whole event became centered on whether or not the persons present liked each other. There was no "public character," as it were, and definition to baptism, which would enable the members of the group to share it in a relatively objective way.

Fifth, there was no cooperative effort in the group to develop suitable analogies that would feed the candidate's understanding of what was going on. When it got bogged down in determining whether baptism was a perpetually ongoing event (which it does not seem to be) or "just a ritual" (in which case, why bother?), the group could easily have drawn on its own significant talent to break that false dilemma. But it did not.

Similarly, when it came to offering a description of Jesus' community that would helpfully differentiate it from other communities one could enter, any publicly available description of that community was neglected in favor of affirming the personal relationship with Jesus that would be involved. The Jesus to whom one would be related did not seem to have any recognizable program other than to love and be friends. Yet the group knew that other people in the world are in favor of love and friendship. In fact, the group seemed embarrassed at the prospect of offering descriptions of itself that might be derogatory to other bodies. Here too conflict had to be avoided, even at the price of making Jesus into little more than a bigger friend, or a friend with connections in high places. The group conveyed to the candidate the idea that this community was one in which we could all be friends with Jesus despite our problems of being friends with one another. In itself this is not a bad description of a Christian community, but it is incomplete, because it does not spell out how friendship among Christians differs, for example, from friendship among Buddhists, animists, or atheists. The program of Jesus is neglected in favor of the person of Jesus.

Sixth, the group seemed to have a problem with relying on others for knowledge about the topic at hand. Such reliance seemed to cause humiliation in the borrower, and for that reason too few people picked up on and improved what others said. They hesitated to offer illustrations, to contradict with historical references, to flesh out with further biblical observations, or even frankly to bypass what was said in favor of another formulation of the matter. It also became clear that *any* formulation was at the same time a matter of leadership, an invitation to others in the group to see the matter from an assumed vantage point. The language circulating in the group was not a neutral thing; it functioned at least partially as an indicator of how much the group had taken measurement of one another and was willing to risk counter-formulation, rebuttal, improvement, or even enthusiastic support. References to Scripture, to liturgical ritual, to traditional doctrine were ambiguous. At times they were introduced to further the work of explanation, and it was only the failure of the group to interact that left these references hanging, as it were, in mid-air, without great explanatory power, conviction or relevance. At other times, however, it seemed that such references were made *rather than* saying something that would further the task. In these instances, they became a pious refuge or an authoritarian way of muscling the candidate or each other, exhortation rather than enlightenment.

* * * * *

What influence did all this have on what got said about baptism by the group? The strongest impression one gets is that *much is unsaid* while the group is doing other business. This is not a negative comment on the group's theological work. On the contrary it is very instructive for our assessment of the group's theological language. One could almost feel how even the most pious, impeccable, revered, and oft-repeated phrases in which baptism was cast called loudly for more explanation, more work, more sense. The group's experience illustrated the more general truth of how difficult it is to raise theological questions—to ask the unsaid—when those questions require creativity, diplomacy, and the ability to monitor static coming from shadow-groups. Yet the group's experience also sets certain directions in which theological questions could be asked and theological observations could be made.

For example, we have an indication of what a daring thing Jesus' baptismal mentality in fact is. Qualities of leadership that can close the distances, real or imagined, between people must be high. The capacity to win trust, and even more to harness that trust to concerted action, must be even higher. That Jesus should make of others baptizers, that he should affirm in them the leadership and capacity to form community by whatever complicated process is required, is an indication of the respect in which he holds others and the confidence he has in them. While he does not view the outset of this process with rose-colored optimism, he credits us with the same stamina to begin that marks his own formation of community. The person who really believes in human community, and believes in God in the midst of human community, possesses a vision and stature that shocks us even as it entices us.

The God of our group (we almost said, "on the other hand") met a varied fate at the group's hands. Some felt, as we saw, that God had not fulfilled the promise of their own baptism. If they were having so much trouble being a community, then what good was their baptism, and what good was his promise to make community out of them? Could even God handle their lack of interaction? Again, God (Jesus, too) was considered to act on such a private, even individualistic, scale that the thought of a God who might have a publicly definable program in mind for mankind was quite absent.

Lastly, any reference to the role of God in the matter of baptism seemed to create much inertia in the group. It was as though the members would have no place to act if God were also acting in the environs. One could only wonder if the group thought the reverse was also true.

III

The
confirmation
group

T I. BACKGROUND*

radition gives us a hodge-podge of confusing data as the basic stuff
of confirmation: imposition of hands, slaps, oil, conferring a name, a
preponderant role of the Holy Spirit, defending the faith, some sort
of strengthening, some close association with baptism, a varying
Church practice (infant confirmation in the East, at a later stage of
life in the West), the confirmational character, a long-standing res-
ervation of this sacrament to the Bishop, and, finally, recent
doctrinal and pastoral descriptions of this sacrament as the sacrament
of Christian adulthood, with strong associations with lay Catholic
action. What we need is a hypothesis that will fit as much of this
traditional data as is possible. Let us suppose, then, that confirmation has something to do with achieving Christian maturity or Christian adulthood.

The first question this raises is how this "Christian maturity"
relates to that secular maturity with which, hopefully, we are more
familiar. The process of human maturing has received much attention in developmental psychology. It is also the theme of much art,
literature, philosophy and daily conversation. Does confirmation
have anything to do with this kind of worldly-wise advance through
cycles of physical, social, personal, and interpersonal growth?

There are certain indications that the tie-in between secular maturing and Christian maturing is closer than we might think. First, there
is the role of the ancient Wisdom literature within the sacred biblical

*See p. 10.

tradition. This wisdom is more often than not of the secular kind. Its very presence in Scripture indicates that such secular maturity is not foreign to man's religious concerns. In fact, it seems to serve as a protection against the heady priestly, legal or prophetic concern that dominate the rest of the scriptural world.[1] The wise man is shrewd, not embarrassed at his own emotions, rarely surprised, an observer of human behavior, particularly of greed and stupidity; he is full of foresight without being careful to a fault. He is ironical, sexually unbiased, though generally harassed by his troubles with women; he has a few thoughts of his own on money, on making friends, and on not getting caught in between.

We all might make up our own version of this kind of profane maturity: the mature person is free to observe fully and accurately what is happening around him as well as to him at the level of personal relations; moreover, he is willing to let most of it happen without too much upset. He has a sense of humor, of whimsy and, at times, of devilment. He enjoys at least some work. He has courage in sickness. He has some good friends of the opposite sex. He is patient, and if necessary unflapable, with the complexity at the root of life. He is aware of and enjoys his bodiliness despite its many problems; he can laugh at its frustrations, and he regrets its gradual breakdown. He is curious about distant places and different horizons. He avoids excessive rationalism. He can distinguish between what can be expected from crowds and what individuals might do. He is slightly confused about it all. He prays once in a while. He likes to see other people change. He appreciates differences in age. He avoids both an urban sophistication and a rural naiveté. He passionately dislikes the killing of human beings. He sees the relative futility of locating blame. He is not too quick to call things a tragedy or a huge success. He can read faces. He recognizes that where he is gifted, it is, after all, a gift. He enjoys the formality of weddings and funerals. He has occasional fits of unconventionality. He hesitates to cooperate in his own torture. He has many warts.

It is this kind of conventional wisdom for which the religious tradition finds ample place in its midst. This fact alone should alert us to a probable connection between the work of confirmation and that growth which is fostered by so many profane sciences.

A second consideration concerning the role of secular maturity within the scope of Christian maturity can be taken from the Gospels themselves. The main points Jesus makes about the Kingdom of God often can not be made to a listener who fails to follow Jesus' observations on secular living: how to deal with a bigger opponent, how fathers act, how to build a house, how the weather is indifferent to people's plans or status, how to store wine, when to move on, how children are basically fickle and how people are basically children, how violence is sometimes necessary, how greedy people are, who gets taxed, how officious middle-men are, how people have double standards.[2] Skimming any one of the synoptic Gospels yields a collection of hard insights like the above. So it seems that some kind of secular wisdom is entailed in Christian maturity, although this does not mean there is nothing specific about the latter.

Very often, in fact, questions about the relationship between secularity and religion are raised in a suspicious manner. If we describe personality development in terminology borrowed from religious sources, we do indeed frequently end up with a clearer understanding of the secular maturing process itself. But to fail to see any differences between the two maturing processes, secular and religious, is, on the face of it, odd. In the one process, we are trying to understand and relate to ourselves and others. This is fine. But in the religious process, we are trying to relate to an invisible, triune God or to a mysteriously risen Jesus. If that does not make for obvious differences, nothing would. The apparent "confusion" between secular and religious maturing seems, then, to mask both a prejudice against and a problem with the spiritual realm which cannot be glossed over. There are basic questions of faith, and of the nature of faith-relationships, which themselves form a separate issue from the issue of secular maturity.

The more central question, however, is "Christian maturity" in itself. Is there any specific *content* of a distinct Christian maturing? Can we isolate and identify that content? The immediate question is not how confirmation achieves this specific maturing, but rather what Christian maturity itself looks like. And in trying to determine what this Christian maturity might be, a caution concerning the use of Scripture is in order. We inevitably bring our prejudices and heuristic questions *to* a reading of Scripture. As a general rule, we find only what we are looking for. When it comes to confirmation, it is usual to look under "Spirit" or "anointing" and leave it at that. It would be more fruitful, however, to approach the Scriptures with this in mind: are there issues that Jesus raises for his followers that move them beyond an initial stage of membership and that belong to a new or second level which can be called a maturer posture within his circle? Bringing this question to a reading of Scripture yields, we suggest, a much fuller and more finely nuanced picture of what the content of Christian maturity might be.[3]

Accordingly, the issues involved in Christian maturity might be formulated like this: (1) How does the disciple assess the time it takes for the Kingdom to arrive? (2) How does the disciple view the inevitability or desirability of suffering for the Kingdom? (3) How does the disciple assess the relationship between law and promise, or that independence from law that is often required by love? (4) How does the disciple assess leadership, authority, prestige within his own community? (5) How does the individual disciple of Jesus exist publicly, that is, as a member of a community that has a public existence as community among other communities in the world? Does his sincerity, discipleship, or devotion to Jesus guarantee that he can meet the special demands of such public existence? How does the disciple deal with those operating outside his own tradition? How does he find the resources to witness to others? (6) What is the disciple's attitude toward the radical freedom of the Father to love according to preference, making the measure of his gifts to mankind his own generosity rather than "the will of the flesh" or "the will of man"? Is God's freedom trustworthy if it is choosey and preferential, elective and selective? (7) How does the community deal with the pluralism in its midst? (8) How does the disciple preserve the uniqueness and centrality of Jesus to the whole operation?

In this light, Jesus himself becomes the ultimate scandal for Christian maturity. That the universe should revolve around him, that he should be so special to the Father, that God in any way should condition or channel or specify his love for *us* in Jesus, all this takes us far beyond an initial contact with Jesus. Yet this very phenomenon has to do with our maturing. We discover that God's action in Jesus is an anticipation, a model of what happens in ourselves. We learn that we, too, are loved and thereby freed *to love*. We too are chosen, selected, endowed, talented and constituted in all *our* uniqueness by an originating love for us in which we are cherished, valued, prized, and esteemed as radically worthwhile. The major part of our maturing lies in accepting this fact. It is Jesus' concern to lead us to such acceptance of what is already and preeminently the truth in his own person. Only then are we equipped to make our personal value public, to reveal fully and overtly that we are "sons" and have the right to act that way. The ancient paradox is there: we grow up to the extent that we see ourselves as children, dependent upon Life, favored by It, sharing It with others.

* * * * *

For each of these maturity-issues a wealth of scriptural materials could be assembled both from the earlier and later strata of the scriptural tradition. The important thing is that some content emerges which might serve to identify a specifically Christian maturity. It is a content which takes us far beyond an initial contact with Jesus and his company. We are into deep water. The situation calls for a second look. The future is more freighted than we might have expected. Things must be measured now with a little more soberness and exactitude. We review the state of our equipment, and make choices about moving ahead.

Like all choices there is an ominous quality about confirmation that suffuses what is in fact something quite simple. For confirmation deals with the *beginning* of Christian maturity. It is the first step in a long process of Christian maturing. The person who is confirmed could hardly, at the point of beginning, be expected to see the content of Christian maturity clearly. He would be fortunate even if he had a vague outline of the issues involved. More would be expected of the Christian community which does the confirming. But even they, though they themselves have been confirmed, will be only on the way toward Christian maturity. The issue is whether or not confirmation is to be seen as a beginning.

This is not as simple as it sounds. For a beginning is among the hardest things to appreciate for what it is: terribly important, but just a start; or the start of terribly important activities. Beginnings must be clearly demarcated from what follows, although it is usual that they are inflated beyond imagining because of the threatening content of that of which they are the beginnings. We can identify a sensibility appropriate to beginnings from a list like the following:

> the first day at a new job
> entering into a room full of strangers
> joining in a parade line
> meeting the other conspirators for the first time
> starting to plow at one end of a huge field
> heading off on a world cruise
> "this is your new home" (to an orphan)
> earning the first dollar in a new business
> being introduced to a famous person

> being shown the secret hiding place
> striding into the middle of an angry mob
> going into the hospital for a biopsy
> joining the flood fighters on the levee
> entering the gates for a long prison term
> starting down a famous art gallery corridor
> taking the field before the big game
> sliding behind the wheel for a long drive
> deciding to give up smoking
> starting to climb an alp
> beginning a diet

getting to the Christmas cards
the first swing in a fight
standing in the door for the jump
wading into the Channel
throwing away the crutches
discovering that you might love someone
meeting the person who will give you the transplant
opening fresh decks at the start of a long poker night

Each of these is at once much and little. In some cases there is an immediacy to the follow-up. In others, that sequel is protracted. In most it would be disastrous to confuse the beginning with the process itself or with the final results. In every case the weight of the projected events impinges on the beginning, coloring it, emotionally challenging it to retain its real proportions. In every case, too, the specific nature of the activity in question is the determining factor in the pressure put upon the beginning. In confirmation, there is much confusion about the beginning. This is partly due to the lack of immediacy to the follow-up, which in turn is due to the almost total lack of explicit awareness of the specific nature of *what* is being begun by confirmation. On the other hand, with explicit awareness comes specific responsibility. And that might be our key problem with confirmation.

II. THE GROUP EVENT

Our overall task is to study how our being in a group
influences what eventually gets said about God,
Jesus, sacraments, or, especially in this case,
the sacrament of confirmation.
To this end the group is to confirm
one of its members, with the proviso that it first
shares the responsibility of explaining
to the candidate what is thereby involved.

This group had observed a previous group at work on a different sacrament, and had commented on the lack of interaction in the previous group. As a result, they came determined not to fall into the same trap. How successful they were is another question. The group began with the question, "Who is going to be the candidate?" The next voice heard was that of a mature woman announcing that "she was thirteen years old, slightly behind her classmates in receiving confirmation, into ballroom dancing and ice-skating, and prejudiced against the soldier-of-Christ motif." The group welcomed her, saying that, just as we had to grow in normal life, so too the life of faith has "a kind of growth." Rose, the candidate, expressed surprise that confirmation had to do with furthering "normal growth" *(which was **not** the point made by the group).* No one took her up on this, so that right from the beginning the issue of Christian-maturity-in-itself was, so to speak, skirted.

The facilitator asked the group whether it might be abandoning its responsibility for the task by the way it let a candidate with so many fictions to her make-up be selected. The picture of a mature woman posing as a thirteen year old seemed suspicious. This became apparent when the next step by the group was to grill Rose about what **she** was looking for from confirmation. *The group was not yet reacting to each other, but was funneling its remarks to each other through Rose.* It could get away with such procedures if the candidate was young enough. So the facilitator suggested that the choice of the fictitious thirteen year old was intentional.

In very halting fashion the group was nonetheless saying to Rose at this point that confirmation had something to do with a growth in faith. However, the growth in faith envisaged by the group was defined as "a greater independence and choice" on the part of the candidate. *The group itself was manifesting neither of these qualities at this point as far as its own behavior went.* The most they would say about their own role was that they were confirming the choice to become more mature that was already going on in the candidate, even though one member told the candidate that, given her age, she was probably being forced to come to confirmation.

Sam pressed Rose on how she could come into this situation "without any prior preparation." Sam was surprised that the candidate's "teacher" could send her there so uninstructed. Whereupon the facilitator *(taking Sam's remark as referring to himself)* asked the group who actually did send the candidate into her role? Of course they did. He also repeated his observation that the group was interrogating the candidate on a grand scale, and again asked whether that was not the reason they had allowed the thirteen-year-old fiction in the first place.

This produced a long discussion in the group about people's difficulties in applying confirmation in any sense to someone who already **is** an adult. It seemed "less real", said Sally. Sam argued that it was no less real than explaining baptism to an adult. The group remained confused about the possibility of confirming someone who was already adult. The facilitator remarked that the whole premise the group was operating on seemed to be that confirmation was an act of the candidate, with no reference to it being an act of the confirming group. If they could not explain confirmation to themselves, it little mattered what age-group they might be dealing with.

At this Rose expressed her own discomfort in the thirteen-year-old role (which she called an "improvisation from experience"). She therefore withdrew her candidacy. Some time passed before the group found another candidate. This turned out to be Sam, who said, "I guess I'm it by default."

Sam spoke the truth. He had assumed leadership earlier by his mild criticism of the facilitator; he was the only one besides the facilitator to object to the fiction of the thirteen-year-old girl; he was subsequently to keep the group honest in its task by not accepting explanations which failed to explain. After the session Sam admitted that the reason he took over as candidate was that he felt sorry for the group because it could not get off the ground. *To help save it, Sam took a role similar to the facilitator's, somewhat outside the group* [the candidate would not have the task of explaining confirmation to himself], *that also placed him in a position to criticize what got said.*

The new candidate began by asking the group whether its confirmation differed in any way from the reception of the Spirit in a pentecostal group. He was immediately lectured on the fact that the sacrament was "an entirely different affair," in which one became "close to the Holy Spirit" and had "great love of God." One could afterwards "pray in the inner depths of the soul," which, before confirmation, was "in its early stages." Sally did not like these claims. For her confirmation was not a prerequisite to maturity, but rather a **recognition** by the community of a growth **already** taking place in the confirmee. This did not satisfy Sam, who asked whether spiritual growth is **at all** conditional upon confirmation.

Marie then gave testimony to what she thought confirmation had contributed to her personally, that she was somehow empowered to be decisive, to take stands out of conviction, to make her voice count. This kind of detail did not seem to Sam to have much to do with God, nor any necessary connection with confirmation. Whereupon Marie advised Sam that he would have to "figure out for himself" what confirmation should be in his Christian life. When Sam added that the fervor and consolation provided by pentecostals seemed to make confirmation superfluous, he was told that, "the things of God cannot be measured and we must accept the need for confirmation on faith."

The group continued to insist that, although their reception of confirmation "did not mean much at the time," they were now inclined to attribute to it much of their subsequent development. Their whole argument was based on personal testimony and personal experience. The facilitator hinted that that might be why they were failing to impress the candidate. *Rather than explaining confirmation, they were subtly forcing Sam to accept **them** in their personal expe-*

rience. Perhaps this explains why Sam indulged in a peculiar form of punishing the group at this point. He urged the group to **continue** piling up the personal testimony; he asked them, yes, to tell him what confirmation did for each of them. And, as each person continued to attribute glowing effects ("strength to do things for people, to risk oneself in social issues, to penetrate to new understanding") to what they said was "just a ritual," Sam kept saying that these same effects could have been achieved without confirmation. Hence, attributing them to confirmation might be just a pious posture.

The group began to work harder to say something specific about what was going on in confirmation. Marie suggested that confirmation entailed some kind of **further insertion into the Christian community.** Tom, despite misgivings about his lack of choice and of understanding at the time of his own confirmation ("I knew I was laying it on the line, but I didn't know **what** I was laying on the line"), saw some need of a **formalized proclamation in ritual** of his desire to get serious. Rose saw confirmation as the individual's **taking on responsibility to grow,** and the community's taking on responsibility to **help** the individual grow. Sally preferred to think of confirmation as **the community's support at a moment** when the individual needs help in affirming Christ's values. Sam parried these offerings, though not without distorting some of them. *The group failed to shake off Sam's increasingly negative leadership, so they were left with the bitter alternative:* either confirmation did nothing, or it simply pepped a person up in ways that could be achieved without it.

The facilitator therefore asked the group if they were avoiding at all costs the topic of "growth in the Spirit." Were they afraid to face the nitty-gritty issue of spiritual maturity *versus* spiritual immaturity? The immediate response to this intervention was an appeal to the "mystery" of confirmation, "which takes its effect no matter when one receives it." Tom was grieved by the language of maturity-immaturity. He would prefer to speak more positively of "fulfillment." He noted that even Jesus' disciples, who rubbed shoulders with him for a long time, needed the additional help of the Spirit to reach fulfillment. The group, rather than pursue this question of language, let the discussion revert to whether confirmation produces what it does produce "mysteriously." Sam continued to press them to explain **how** confirmation was so special or different. A feeble effort was made to attribute to confirmation "our present ability to work together despite a great pluralism." *Sadly, this was the very quality that was lacking in the group at that moment.*

Finally, when Sam said that "even a crew working together at Cape Canaveral had such an ability," *the group's anger turned on him.* He was asked to state what **he** was bringing to the community's general level of maturity, "since he alluded so often to his own maturity." Sam simply denied having done so, stating that, whatever the state of his maturity, it did not seem to need confirmation either in its origin or in its continuation. *The anger, however, was revealing. No one, including Sam, up to that point had even admitted in principle the distinction between mature and immature. Yet it was obviously on everyone's mind.* At any rate, shortly after this flare-up there was a spontaneous movement in the group to agree that the "fulfillment" language it had used earlier was perhaps too nice. "Decisions could be mature without seeming very fulfilling." *The group was beginning to feel the topic of maturity now,* but without defining it and without any shared anchor for its feelings.

At this point, Sam, *relenting somewhat in his stance toward the group,* asked it what it saw as the role of the Spirit in confirmation. This time, however, Sam urged them to draw from their own experience **or from the Church at large** to spell out the Spirit's role. The possibility that there could be such an objective (beyond this immediate group) view of the Spirit had not yet been aired. A previous intervention of the facilitator ("When the Spirit comes, is he allowed to have anything specific on his mind?") had been completely ignored. *The group still had great apprehension at learning from each other, reacting to each other or showing their talent.* So when Sam started carping at their most recent offerings concerning the Spirit's role in confirmation, *their frustration level reached a new high.* "You believe in the Spirit among pentecostals," Sam was told, "why not in confirmation?" Nevertheless, the group tried valiantly to work out the differences between pentecostal baptism and confirmation. They assigned a certain activity and vibrancy to pentecostals. Since all pentecostals had, after all, been confirmed, perhaps that might even explain their vibrancy. Another suggestion was lost in the group, namely, that they should consider confirmation from the perspective of it including the bishop, which pentecostal baptism does not expressly do.

The facilitator felt that the group was flying away from the issue of maturity-immaturity. So he asked whether the group was hesitating to call pentecostals immature. Marie said that she thought they were immature. Her remark was immediately buried by the group, until the facilitator asked again if the group was shying away from calling any behavior immature because that would be dangerous. A long silence followed, whereupon someone said, "Well, no one called anything immature, did they?" To which the answer came, "Yes, Marie just did." Marie, then, began to expand on her statement, saying that pentecostals did not exhibit enough doubt at the center of their faith to make her feel comfortable. With this beginning the session ended.

III. THEOLOGICAL IMPLICATIONS

The foregoing exercise illustrates how the desire to keep things nice sometimes deters a group from performing a task of theological explanation with the clarity and concentration that is desirable. But there is more to the matter than a self-defeating gentility. A great tension existed in the group as to what might offend other persons present. There was very little, if any, mutual correction; there was little negotiation about accepting this or that expression as the practical consensus of the group; an individual's suggestions were not taken up by others and plumbed for their best implications. The confirmation group wanted badly to do these things. They wanted badly to relate to each other, to God, to the Spirit, to the candidate, to Jesus—to *anyone* who was "a person." But by this relating they frequently meant a kind of mindless acceptance, an easy and assured relationship with enthusiasm, stimulation, and camaraderie. Yet, this hope for festivity was belied by the strain present as they tried to keep together *both* their concern for persons *and* their common task of explaining confirmation.

We can learn from their experience. Who we are as persons does not exist in a void apart from what we are and what we are about. Rather, the moment we talk about this "what," we seem to put "who" we are on the line. We give definition to our person through our choices; that is why choice is so perilous and dramatic. But choices are made not only by some*one;* they are made by someone choosing to do some*thing*. In a group the "things" add up, so we wonder whether there is room for *what* everyone wants to do and to choose. The matter is even more unnerving. Differences as to what is chosen (programs, roles, things-to-do, etc.) also hint at the more radical differences of persons (talents, competences, charisms) involved. The latter seem to be what is really bothering the group, as though another person does not leave my person room *by his or her very personhood*. This conflict of persons is always expressed through the medium of *what* someone does or says or proposes or values. But in any case the potential for disruption in a group is great.

The *growth* of persons, too, is measured in part by what is done by them, by the phases or stages or experiences or forms of behavior they pass through. Patterns of action leading to maturity are traced back to the person, so that some persons are called mature while others are not. It is true that socio-cultural influences are significant in deciding what constitutes such maturity. But the person who wants to be called mature apart from *any* such assessment of behavior we would usually call omnipotent or childish. We know that our maturing is tied to *some* forms of behavior (however unsure we are of *which* forms), and we live in dread of failing to pass at the judgment seat of maturity. These same concerns operate, we suggest, when the topic is Christian maturity. Perhaps that is why we try to live with such a vague picture of confirmation.

The presuppositions of the group concerning the Holy Spirit are also instructive. To them the Spirit meant vibrancy, enthusiasm, power—all of which, by the way, seemed to be lacking both in their group-life and in their pursuit of the theological task. It was hard for them to express to the candidate the Spirit's role in confirmation.

In its basic imagery, "spirit" can say many things. It connotes the strength of a gale, or the dull, repetitive breathing which is a sign of life's presence, or the arbitrariness and fickleness of the wind, or heaving anger or enthusiastic breathlessness. In the Old Testament the Spirit of Jahweh sometimes has one or other of these anthropomorphic overtones. More often we are dealing with the spiritual activity and interchange of God with men. Men and women receive in the Spirit missions (e.g., as judges, prophets, lawgivers, priests, etc.) from Jahweh which will further his saving plans for the world. The emphasis is upon action.

In the New Testment there is a movement toward interiority. The Holy Spirit is present in Jesus' work and person in a strangely permanent way,[4] without losing his familiar unsettling "style." It is in the Spirit that one learns to converse familiarly and easily with the Father, as his sons.[5] It is in the Spirit that one begins to see things through the Father's eyes, gaining his tastes and sensibilities, making his kind of judgements on things and people and situations.[6] But in addition to providing this psychological attunement to the Father, the Spirit in the New Testament is also lawyer, arguer, convincer, debater.[7] He stands by the Christian's side and whispers to him what to say, when to keep his mouth shut, how to stay calm. He has his sheaf of arguments, his dossiers, his gestures of accusation and indignation. He brings all things back to the issue of Jesus, around whom the Great Case centers.

Despite this tradition, our group acted as though God could *never* be associated with argument, contradiction or debate. And "the Spirit of confirmation" could *never* need definitions, facts, clarification of issues, checking whether something was or was not compatible with Jesus, and so on. Much of this might reflect the group's struggle with its own life rather than its theological views. The Spirit, who is described as chrism or soothing balm, seems at times to be invoked as the balm of the group itself as it is torn by its own lack of sharing and its disagreements. But there is a great deal of carry-over to what gets said about confirmation and about the Spirit of God in confirmation.

Here, as in the baptism group, the group was having difficulty seeing itself as confirmers. Why define what one is not authorized, in the larger Church, to do? The group felt powerless to be confirmers. This tends to make it look as though their whole problem stemmed from their being treated immaturely in the Church. But this is not the whole of the matter.

Hovering over the session is one especially vivid question about God: How do we sort out what belongs to God's agency from what belongs to ours? How does one cooperate with God? The group comes back often to the view that confirmation is some kind of divine empowering. While God's empowering might well be central to the theology of confirmation, more seems to be going on as the group discusses it. First, the group is highly conscious of power failures and power struggles within its own group-life. These sentiments are particularly painful in the context of a confirmation. For, where the premise is accepted that confirmation has something to do with maturity, the presence of violence, frustration, paralysis, jealousy, and powerlessness is embarrassing. There is also question of the power of theological explanation in the group, whether anyone is really convinced or persuaded by anyone else. Secondly, the issue of power is touched in the group's manifest attitudes toward their own past confirmation. Some seemed to feel that they had been violated by their own confirmation, overpowered in the sense of having been brought into something whose dimensions they really did not understand, however benevolently they accepted it. Thirdly, guilt over the two previous realizations makes the group hesitant to take anything like a power-stance toward the candidate. How *dare* it confirm the candidate if it is not itself mature? How *could* it overpower the candidate by doing to him what had been done to itself?

Fourthly, besides this sense of guilt, there is a good deal of fear and self-doubt in the group about its own creative resources. Sam was such a powerful leader that the group could hardly pretend it was hurting him very much. But if it was not hurting him, if he really was so powerful, where would it get the ability to provide him with a good catechesis of confirmation? The group seems almost visibly relieved whenever the case is made in it for the candidate's already having achieved adulthood, Christian or otherwise. For then there will be no need for the group to draw on its own resources to provide the candidate with an adult explanation of confirmation. An even weaker reaction of the group to its own fear is to let the candidate define for it what confirmation is all about. This abandoning by the group of its responsibility has a temporarily pleasant effect. The candidate is comfortable, if slightly embarrassed, in dictating his terms to the group. But he is also somewhat puzzled at being let off so easily.

Fifthly, in the midst of its guilt and fears, the group can take some powerfully destructive paths: It can put impossible or unlikely demands on the candidate which serve only to frighten him (the candidate must be responsible, adult, committed, clearheaded, motivated, etc.). This approach usually looks silly to the group after a while. (As one member finally commented, "Well, has *anyone* ever been refused this sacrament?" Another member described how, in a parish, a young boy was asked by the Bishop according to the usual formality whether he wished to be confirmed. To everyone's astonishment, the boy answered in a clear voice, "No." The Bishop, thinking he must have misheard him, confirmed the young boy anyway.) Or the group can promise the candidate the works, telling him that confirmation will provide him with explosive power as a witness. It can neglect to make any mention of failure in the pursuit of maturity, which is the fate of most of us.

* * * * *

No wonder, then, that the empowering of God is on everyone's mind. At the same time, the group's experience cautions us to observe critically what kind of "power" is being attributed to God, both in general and in the case of confirmation. Is it the power to escape the kind of painful interactions that occur in the group? Is it a power which leads to or underscores our guilt and failure? Is it a power that points with pride at our powerlessness? Or is it a power which raises us to its own omnipotent status? Is it a mindless power, or does it set us sensible and manageable tasks? Is it power bent on success at all costs? Is God's power free, in such wise that confirmation can be a "special arrangement" on God's part? We have seen the group at times stress the view that God is *continuously* at work in a human life, even before confirmation. On the surface, the view seems flattering to God. But we have also seen how such a view tends to make confirmation superfluous. The group cannot conceive of God freely making any "new steps" or "special arrangements," because everything that God ever does is always so good and effective. Yet, behind the flattery the group is often wrestling with a more basic problem it has with God's power: "How can we be taking this new, special step of confirming someone, when all power, as it always has, rests with God anyway?"

IV

The
penance
group

T I. BACKGROUND*

he sacrament of penance is, in its most obvious features, a conversation between an official of the Christian community and another person about the sins of the latter. Some people "undergo" this conversation not for any intrinsic merits of its own, but because they see it as the means of obtaining God's forgiveness. It might even appear to them to be a rather arbitrary condition set down by God to that end. They certainly feel that outside of this conversation forgiveness is generally unavailable. In their understanding, God remains opposed to the sinner until the sinner has deposited his sins, as it were, at the proper place. The nature of sin is offered as the reason for this procedure: as offense against God, it can be removed only on God's terms. And the idea seems to be that what is important to God is that the sinner humbly own up to his sin to another human being who is authorized to mediate God's forgiveness. This human contact also *happens* to be psychologically good for him, but the main issue is God's forgiveness, no disrespect to psychology intended. Given the proper capitulation on the sinner's part, and given this ritual conversation, God will relent. Without them either his hands are tied, or his omnipotent mood would have to change greatly.

If the preceding picture seems like a caricature of the sacrament of penance, it is not too great a distortion of what many people recount as their experience of it. Put the matter another way. We can consider all the possible forgiving relationships that the sinner can enter into. He can be forgiven (1) by God, (2) by a Church official, or

*See p. 10.

the god of the group

(3) by individual Christians (or any individual, for that matter) whom he has offended or who encounter him as a sinner. The view of the sacrament we are criticizing here is one in which the sole reason for contact with a Church official (2) is to attain God's forgiveness (1).

One problem with this view is that it very subtly places the forgiveness of sin within the dubious framework of a kind of testing of God. Each time the issue is posed: Will God be forgiving as I go through this conversation? And each time, everything depends on my success in performing this conversation correctly. Moreover, by insisting that it was God, after all, who made such a conversation the condition for his forgiveness, we give the impression that the whole problem of forgiveness resides with God. The sacrament becomes an inexorable prelude to God's forgiveness. It also becomes a frightening experience, since anything else is certainly going to take second place to this dramatic encounter with a hesitant God.

Yet, the issue of whether or not God *will be* forgiving is, in the light of the Christian tradition, a red herring, and a gigantic diversion. It is a game which shifts the problem from where it is (whether *we* will be forgiving to one another) to where it is not (whether God will be forgiving). It is not as though the forgiveness of God is in *no* way involved in this sacrament. But *how* that forgiveness operates is another matter entirely. For the present, we suggest that God's forgiveness normally operates in the sacrament as the source and creative force for all the *other* forgiving that goes on. His *personal* forgiving of an individual awaits only that individual's repentence, which may or may not coincide with the reception of the sacrament. To imagine that God's forgiving is timed to the ritual expression of the sinner's sorrow is neither traditional, necessary, nor useful. Our own personal habits, attitudes and experience of being forgivers could tell us much in this matter. They might explain why we talk about God's forgiveness the way we often do, making it so fitful and controlled.

It is possible to find in Scripture itself this tendency to make God the problem in the forgiveness of sins. An incident related by the snynoptics[1] has the scribes commenting on Jesus' act of forgiving the paralytic, "Who can forgive sins but God?" Pious tradition has often concluded from this incident that Jesus must be claiming here to be God. Unfortunately, to do so is to miss the point of the whole incident. First, it is the villains of the piece whose interpretation we would be accepting. Secondly, it is nowhere apparent that Jesus is invoking his divine status in the incident. On the contrary, his point is to prove the scribes wrong. To do so, he shows that *he* will forgive sins, and he will argue that doing so is *easier* than curing a paralytic. The reason why Jesus characterizes the attitude of the scribes as

48

"wicked thoughts" seems precisely because they are hiding behind their principle in order to avoid a task that *is* in their power.

The general and preponderant behavior and teaching of Jesus bear this out: not only should men forgive each other's sins, but *if they do not, neither will God*. It would be odd to cast Jesus in the very volatile role of saying, on the one hand, "you have the responsibility to forgive," and, on the other, of saying, "remember, only God can forgive." Yet, this is what is frequently done. *Authorization* is substituted for *responsibility* as the issue of forgiveness. And once this happens it is a short step to make God the scapegoat in the whole affair, wondering whether he in fact will authorize a particular act of forgiving.

The reaction of the onlookers in the scriptural incident described above is interesting. They too had trouble concentrating on the point Jesus was making. They confess having seen something wonderful; they praise God; they are filled with awe and astonishment; they acknowledge the power of God. Such fixation on God (though in the narration it has no doubt more to do with the physical cure involved) is easily a distraction from Jesus' *denial* of the Pharisaic principle that only God can forgive sins.

The issue of God's authorization, then, can be a dodge from our own responsibility. One wonders how another classical text is read, "Whose sins you shall forgive, they are forgiven; whose sins you shall retain, they shall be retained."[2] Again we are dealing with a text that has been interpreted almost completely in terms of authorization. But it is possible to miss the more probable sense (in the context of Jesus' constant exhortation to be responsible forgivers), "If *you* do not forgive sins, how will sinners be forgiven when they confront *you?* If *you* hold back, the sinner is held back, because that is where the issue is being met."

The record of God on forgiveness is clear. God's fixed and continual stance is to be forgiving. In Paul's unambiguous, jarring and awesome language, it is God's way to acquit the guilty.[3] So much for justice. It is this awareness, more than anything else, that is to draw the sinner away from sin to repentance. All God seems to want is that the sinner be sorry for sin. And this, not only because sin is a nasty and unworthy business, but also lest God seem to bring his forgiveness to bear on someone who does not wish it, which would be very impolite as we know from our own experience of forgiving. For the rest, God's stance is predictable. It anticipates the sinner's repentance. It supports every effort at forgiveness by men. God's forgiveness is better, smoother, more sensitive, more generous and more reasonable than any we could devise.

Perhaps a simpler explanation for the fixation on God's role in the sacrament of penance is the desire people have for *certain* knowledge of his *guaranteed* forgiveness of them as *individuals*. We have to ask, however, whether such a desire is at all legitimate. Even if it were, we have to ask whether the *sacrament* of penance is intended to provide for *it*. To do this, we must first say something about how sacraments in general embody the grace or favor of God. This overall view of God's way of dealing in the sacraments might explain why some of the demands we put on God in the sacrament of penance are misplaced.

The favor of God is not vague or global. His love is not simply a diffuse mood or affectivity or reassurance. By grace specific things happen, develop or are anticipated. Creation, which is the primal grace, demonstrates this point very well: things spring up in all their individuality and concreteness. Creation also reminds us that the chief characteristic of God's favor is precisely its creational power. When the favor of God is involved, things are brought into being. Without that favor, nothing literally is. Conversely, the favor is literally to make things to be.

In the case of the sacraments, what comes into being is not some third quantitative "thing" (besides the loving God and besides the sacramental action being performed) called "grace." Rather, sacraments *are themselves* the favor God does us. The favor of God is that we *be* baptizers, confirmers, forgivers and forgiven, and so on. These specific activities are what comes into being by God's free and creative power. They are the sacramental grace that God gives. Our difficulty in seeing this, our tendency to alienate from ourselves the real grace of the sacraments and to substitute another, vaguer one, stem in part from our ambivalence toward the activities themselves. Is it a favor to us that we be forgiving? That we be baptizers? That we be critical of standards of love? All these are demanding activities. Do we really believe the one who gets us into them is doing us a favor?

The matter is complicated by the fact that God's sacramental favor to us is not an all-at-once affair. Our performance of the sacraments is but the start of his sacramental grace. In addition, God *promises* to make us forgivers, to make us mature, and so forth, in an *ongoing* fashion. So we are always waiting for the promise to take full effect. What we have is a gracious, astonishing, freely offered promise from God, of which the sacramental action is, as it were, the first fruits. But waiting makes us nervous, especially since we know that God's favors to us do not rob us of our freedom to accept them or not at any point along the line.

Let us try to imagine this sacramental promise of God further. In our ordinary experience we are familiar with what we call formal promises. A teacher, for example, can make a formal commitment to set aside several *extra* hours each week for student interviews. He is doing this as a favor. But formal promises are not exclusive. They do not mean that a person cannot act outside of the situation covered by the promise. He is still quite open and ready to deal with students at any time on an informal basis. Neither do they mean that he will act differently in the period promised. The teacher is not necessarily going to be smarter, more eager, more loving, or more successful during the times when he is acting on his formal promise. In fact, it would be insulting to think so. His generosity should not be mistaken for a panacea or for magic. The nature, quality, and process of his helping is not necessarily changed by the formality of his promise to help. But that is not what people expect. Either they forget the freedom of his original formal promise, confusing it with something *owed* them, or they fantasize that he wishes to deal with them *only* in such circumstances (forgetting his more extensive commitment to informal dealings), or they expect marvels to occur when they do consult him within the promised times. In short, people are people.

To apply this image of formal promise to God's favor in the sacraments is our next step. We are suggesting that God brings Christians together to do specific activities called sacraments. What we believe these activities are, we try to make clear in the rest of this book. Our view implies a "formal promise" on his part to lend his creativity to people in an ongoing way as they engage in the activities involved in the sacraments. The formal promise is what it is, nothing more, nothing less. Because it is a free promise, we should stand in awe and gratitude for it. We should realize that the promises of God bear on the very existence of things, so that without that promise nothing comes to be. But we should not therefore forget that God also deals in informal settings. We cannot say that, whereas he is trustworthy when his formal promises are concerned, we should be cautious about his behavior outside of those circumstances. Nor should we expect panaceas or magic from those situations in which we come into contact with his formal promises.

But, being people, we do all of this to his formal promises. We distort them to satisfy our own demands for assurance, guaranteed success, controlled access (of whom to whom?) and exaggerated protocol. The sacraments are important, but they are peripheral activities in God's general conduct of the world. Their importance is underscored by the formality of God's promise in their case. But they can easily be made too much of.

Nowhere are these attitudes towards sacraments in general more prevalent than in the sacrament of penance. The situation is emotionally disruptive. The "future" of the sinner as sinner seems to be at stake. Past habits set the probabilities for future outcomes. Our resourcefulness for virtue seems scanty. We frequently do not even understand why we might be recounting our tale of shame and woe to this official of the Church. We even wonder whether we are "the Church" in the same way that anyone else is. Have we set someone else's standards up as our own, and thus begun to measure our failures by a false yardstick? In these circumstances, our assessment of the favors being shown us by God in the sacrament of penance is going to be made at the cost of much discipline and concentration.

The tradition of the Church has been that God's sacramental grace attaches to a conversation between sinners and *official* forgivers in the community. Conversations about sin with non-officials have not been called sacramental, at least not until now. It is this very difference created by the presences of the official minister that has added to the confusion concerning the grace of the sacrament of penance.

More needs to be said about this in the chapter on orders, but the following remarks might be helpful here. Our problem is that, just as we make too much or too little of formal promises, so too we make too much or too little of what is official. Worse still, we go on to confuse the two. We talk of God's official forgiveness when we actually mean God's formal promises concerning man's official forgiveness. We equate the officialness of the Church with God (back to the authorization issue), as though God acted only "officially." We look upon officialness as "a formality."

This basically garbled and sceptical attitude towards formality then carries over towards our understanding of God's free promises to us. We wonder, in effect, whether the formal promise of God is good enough to live on. We question whether it offers sufficient motivation to undergo the conditions of official forgiveness to which the tradition has directed us. Above all, we are tested in our faith whether God's formal promises, which seem to be operative in *community* situations, are of any use when community does not seem to exist, or where our individual fate might loom larger to us at a particular moment than any community concern. All of these factors, then, threaten our sense of security with God's promised grace in the sacrament of penance. Where that grace appears so directed, so concrete and specific, *so tied to situations in which we move uneasily,* then and there God becomes the problem of the sacrament of penance.

The theology of the sacrament of penance has to say something about the sin that figures so highly in it. The events, actions and situations that have been called sins from the beginning of time are numberless.

52

What is crucial in the following analysis is that faith and the faith-tradition enter into the matter at the most basic level. They condition, determine, and constitute *what is to pass for sin* in the community.

It is astounding that people often try to identify and locate sin according to criteria that are so personal, arbitrary, uninformed, and generally sloppy that their behavior simply does not come *up* to being "Christian sin." They misappropriate Christian language to describe questionably Christian experience. It is somewhat greedy to claim the name "Christian" for one's conduct *or misconduct* without testing that claim against the Christian tradition.

Louis Monden well describes how one and the same language of Christian morality (conscience, obligation, law, guilt, sin, sorrow, confession) can cover wholly different kinds of behavior, only some of which are envisaged when we speak of Christian sin.[4] His "Instinctual Man" is a haunted figure, subject to abject anxiety before other people's regulations, surrounded by taboos, reacting in automatic fear rather than responding in moral situations. He has little personal freedom or capacity to estimate the *moral* "oughtness" of his actions. Morality is a series of maneuvers aimed at forestalling punishment or at anticipating the plans of others to thwart one's baser desires. And yet, all the "moral" language is used to describe this unfree and fearful existence.

Monden's "Moral Man" is more interested in the cosmetic aspects of morality, that is, "Do I have all my virtues on straight? Am I being consistent with the line of authentic self-development that my conscience calls me to?" Moral Man's integrity is uppermost in his mind. His immorality consists of structural flaws in that integrity. If a man is unfaithful to his wife, the flaw is revealed in his failure to meet a standard governing his personal makeup. The standard is, to be sure, God-given. But this aspect of conscience is secondary. It is the demand of self-fidelity that counts. All his moral working-parts must function according to a built-in pattern of identity and purpose. If he is bad, analogies are to be sought from bad toasters, or bad lawn-mowers, rather than from elsewhere. They do not run the way they should.

Yet is all this what Christians mean by sin? True, the Christian tradition has insisted that personal conscience reveals to an individual what is necessary for his radical moral integrity before God. But the source of moral demands (personal conscience) should not be confused with the shape and content of those demands. If a person's personal conscience calls him to a relationship of love and service to Christ, and if it makes this *relationship* critical for his personal integrity, nevertheless his morality is henceforward to be measured in terms of relationship to that community and relationship with Christ. If something goes wrong, it is now less important that *personal* integrity is lost. What matters is that the *relationship* has been affected negatively. The parties to the relationship therefore share, if you will, the personal conscience of each other, because of the freely given entry established at the outset of the relationship. Morality is no longer a question of ''I,'' but of ''we.''

The language of morality, then, while itself remaining fixed, can mask quite different and fluctuating views of life. The Christian tradition, we suggest, has created several noticeable disruptions in the history of morality, all of which have had a significant effect on what is to pass for sin. Let us consider several of them.

1. At times, the Christian faith has seemed to say that man is so much ''in sin'' that he would have little else to talk about in life save this fact. Understandably, people who have accepted this as the Christian view have preferred to say nothing at all about sin, accepting their good and bad behavior with a sort of fatalism. We are referring of course to the *doctrine of original sin*. In this doctrine it is proposed that the world, without Christ and without the Christian community (a condition, by the way, no longer totally verified), is failing to achieve the full promise which it obviously should achieve. Theoretically the achievement of that promise is available to all, for God has made all beneficiaries of it. But the world is either stalled in its progress toward that promise or is receding from it. Recession and stagnation are not considered here to be the voluntary acts of any individual. Yet they constitute a situation which affects all men, and which has affected all men from the beginning. The predicament is aggravated by the interlocking effect of the numbers of people involved, and by the weight of time. This situation, moreover, is not simply a mess. Given the alternative available—the fact that, according to God's promise, it need not be so—it is a poignant mess. It is a sin, in the normal sense of being an enduring, complicated shame. And, by a logic interior to the situation itself, men will pay for it, if nothing is done about it.[5]

It is important to stress that the God of original sin seems to create the problem by his very largess. By making available to mankind, as a pure gift, familiarity with himself, fraternity with each other, sexual identity and joy, cultural diversity within world unity, creative interaction with the forces of nature, simplicity of heart, and the promise of life hereafter, God seems to look the villain when mankind does nothing to live up to this promise.

People are hardly going to concentrate on the truth that life itself and all life's possibilities are pure gift, are not theirs by right. Any complications, then, that arise along the way are viewed as the fault of the donor. We seem to have received damaged goods. We do not advert to what either we or others (our ancestors, for example) have contributed to the general mess, although in the privacy of our thoughts we know that we have fouled up or someone else has done us in by their conduct. It is our custom, however, to vent our anger on the nearest nice person, since we have confidence that at least *that* person can absorb our venom. In the case of the world's situation, that nice person is God. So that, right from the beginning, any discussion about man's "sinful" situation presents God to us in a highly ambivalent light, as nice and uplifting on the one hand, incompetent or full of tricks on the other.

2. Perhaps this restless and unresolved ambivalence of ours is *what Paul meant when he characterized certain root-sins* in all of us. These root-sins are a disturbing phenomenon in the New Testament. We are all touched by them, but it is not clear how anything permanent ever gets done about them even through contact with the baptismal community. They describe an inner mood or tendency of people. They affect our specific behavior, but are not the same as it.

Bultmann isolates several such root-sins in the New Testament:[6] crowing *(kauchasma),* a sort of loud-mouthed bravura by which we try to assure our cosmic importance; cringing *(phobos)*, whereby we postpone any good work in the name of a vague unworthiness or feigned subservience, and thus save ourselves a lot of trouble all around; covetousness *(epithumia)*, a kind of belligerent lust and possessiveness; carefulness *(merimna)*, in the Irish sense of a "careful" man who gauges all present involvements by what they might entail later on, cautiously keeping track of all potential demands on himself; banking on *(pepoiethenai)* the world, which includes a judgement of reliability and security as well as a choice of allegiance in the face of threatening options. The latter stance masks a radical kind of self-reliance, of trusting in oneself to be able to procure life through one's own accomplishment.

Paul is not always clear about who the other party is in these root-sins. But the foregoing attitudes and sentiments do seem to encompass man's relationship to God. Nor does Paul tell us how conscious of these attitudes the sinner is. In any case, they seem to be a fact of the sinner's life. The proclamation of the gospel entails both highlighting them and then somewhat surmounting them. The faith-tradition keeps the picture of sinful man real. It does not say, "You are beautiful and therefore we will cure you." Neither does it say, "You are ugly by the very fact that you exist." The reality is somewhere in between. The faith-tradition says that our relationship with God is hedged with many unresolved attitudes which need care and confident treatment.

3. Another place where the faith-tradition has an input concerning the meaning of Christian sin is the area of *sinful performance*. Moral

failures are measured against moral possibilities, so it was natural that Christianity would come up with its own view of how human activities are to be classed on a moral scale. The New Testament begins the listing of certain types of actions that are inconsistent with a relationship to God in Christ. Some types of actions, such as adultery, fornication, murder, the oppression of widows and orphans, are clearly immoral in these listings. Other types of actions, such as eating certain foods or observing certain feast days, are the subject of great debate in the New Testament. Principles for maneuvering through the debate are also provided. The greatest of these is man's personal conscience, where he is in most proximate touch with the spiritual direction of God himself.

In subsequent stages of the Christian moral tradition, we encounter the same mixture of firm positions and debated ones. There is this difference, namely, that, with the added dimension of history, the firm positions of one generation often become the debated positions of the next generation. Or what are firm positions in one part of the global village are not so firm in another part of it. Questions are also raised about just how firm is firm: when we are talking about principles, do we mean absolute ones which admit of no exception? Or do we mean general principles which hold for the most part, but do not of themselves exclude every instance of the type of conduct in question? Finally, who says so? The debate concerning the truth or falsity of moral principles is further complicated by the question of who can authoritatively decide moral truth in the Christian community. As arguments over authority increase, so does the debate about principles. More and more, personal conscience is thrown back on its own (God's) authority to proceed morally through life. More and more, the picture of Christian morality becomes one of conflicting personal consciences, some of which are highly placed and authoritatively titled, some of which are not so, but which have nonetheless an influence on the moral consensus of the community at any given period.[7]

* * * * *

This is an all too brief picture of how the Christian community discovers or establishes the standards against which its sins are measured. We cannot even begin to develop the picture here or to illustrate it from specific burning issues of our times. Nor is this the place. Suffice it to say how emotionally loaded these issues are. Under such circumstances, how is personal conscience to act? It is a sensitive mechanism anyway, subject to distortion, rumor, hearsay, fad, compromise, dullness, fawning conformism, alarmist tendencies, self-serving and weepy subservience. It does not wish to be left alone with God. It feels it knows more trustworthy or more worldly-wise counsellors, or, when it comes right down to it, it does not like taking orders much anyhow.

Now when conversations about sin occur in the Christian community, what sin are we talking about? Should people confess as sin their *original sin*—their situation of unfulfilled promise, the complicated odds against them, their creaturely need? This situation admittedly does not constitute personal guilt in them. But people often feel guilty about being dependent on others, or about outrageously generous promises to them that have not been acted upon. Or is it that they feel resentful and therefore guilty? Should one talk about these things? Or are they to be left unsaid, the distant horizon against which more concrete misconduct is silhouetted? Is the sacrament of penance some complaint bureau where we lament our hopeless interdependence with other people's freedom, or where we bemoan our creaturely status and the obvious advantage that this status gives to God? Or is the breathless outpouring of all this woe too great for words?

Are the *root-sins* the subject of remorse and confession? How does one talk about a deep-seated grumble, an attitude or penchant? It is not as though root-sins have an obvious and specific malice, as, for example, an act of lying or of injustice has. They do seem, in Paul's analysis, to be "intentional." But not being what we normally understand as moral misbehavior, what do we say about them? And if they perdure despite everything, do they mock our confession of guilt? Or does talking about them help?

Should we confess having violated someone else's principles? For, in the flurry of *competing claims to moral truth,* the one Christian community does not always agree in conscience that this type of action is absolutely immoral, or that type of action is even generally immoral. Yet there seems to be an unspoken pressure to confess sin according to some prevailing consensus about sin in the community, or according to some statistical majority, or according to some official list of sins (which may or may not be up to date). How much moral acuity and sophistication—what used to be called "serious matter, sufficient reflection and full consent of the will"—is presupposed in the conversation of the sacrament of penance? And what kind of relationship to Christ is needed to provide even the possibility of sins against *that* relationship? The sacrament of penance seems to create that relationship as much as it presupposes it, but the process is extremely delicate. The risk of talking about morality instead of about personal sin is high. The fear of exposing a personal conscience that conflicts with accepted moral positions, conservative or liberal, is always present. This is especially the case when the other party to the conversation, the minister, is an official of the community. That association identifies him with the public moral stances of the community. To be sure, the community believes first and foremost in personal conscience. It believes that a person sins through personal conscience and personal conscience alone. But talk about the legitimacy and scope of personal conscience is not the loudest to be heard from the community's official platform. So the presence of the official in this conversation can even block us from seeing how this can be a conversation about real sin, Christian sin.

A further difficulty surrounds the presence of a Church official in this conversation. The popular complaint runs, "Why do I have to confess to a priest rather than to the person I have offended? Why do I have to get God's forgiveness from him?" There is a poignant illogic in the complaint. Beneath its simple exterior, many things are being said. Notice the "have to," and explore its implications. Are we back to God-the-problem? Notice the suspicious optimism about confessing to the person who has been offended. Notice the absence of any reference to the community, even though the priest is obviously acting here as an official of the community. For, in fact, it is not "forgiveness" that is involved in this conversation, but *this* forgiveness from *this* official. We would almost expect next a protestation to the effect that the sinner would prefer to confess openly to the community at large and be forgiven by them. Not a bad idea in itself, as we shall see. But when faced with that prospect, the sinner can only ask: Will they be forgiving? So the question boils down to what the official's forgiving might have to do with the community at large and what the sinner might have to do with the community at large. Let us consider the last point first.

More is at stake here than any question of justice due the community. It is customary to explain the community's involvement with the sinner in this way: because any sin affects the community, the community deserves to be consulted (through its minister), and the sinner should have the decency to do so. There is some truth to this argument, but it is not the whole explanation. The community is there *for* the sinner. It is there to care for the sinner's real needs. What are these needs?

The most basic desire of people is to be themselves before the world. We want to show our true selves, to fully and publicly exist as we are. We want to throw off pretense and convention, subterfuge and enforced disguise. It is not that we cannot support intricate and artful facades. We are only too good at them. But we are not taken in by them. We do not want to be the puppeteers at our own dumb-show. Bonhoeffer's poetry expresses well this tension between a public and private self:

> Am I then really all that which other men tell of?
> Or am I only what I myself know of myself?
> Restless and longing and sick, like a bird in a cage,
> Struggling for breath, as though hands were compressing my throat,
> Yearning for colors, for flowers, for the voice of birds,
> Thirsting for words of kindness, for neighborliness,
> Tossing in expectation of great events,
> Powerlessly trembling for friends at infinite distance,
> Weary and empty at praying, at thinking, at making,
> Faint, and ready to say farewell to it all?
>
> Who am I? This or the other?
> Am I one person today and tomorrow another?
> Am I both at once? A hypocrite before others,
> And before myself a contemptibly woebegone weakling?
> Or is something within me still like a beaten army,
> Fleeing in disorder from victory already achieved? [8]

This thirst for openness is especially present in the matter of our sinful selves. We long for some means of identifying ourselves to the world as sinners. Like Oedipus, we have a faint realization that the sickness of the city comes back in part to ourselves. We have carried the plague into our town. We would like to say so, but we fear the consequences. The laugh, the sneer, the I-told-you-so, the vengeance, the tag of unreliability—these make us recoil back on ourselves, where we remain enclosed.

The Christian community wants things to be otherwise. It is convinced that Jesus wanted to create an atmosphere in which sin can be expressed *because* a favorable hearing can be presumed. The burden on the community is to create this atmosphere for forgiving. It should show by its behavior that the wall between God and sinners is already broken down. It should take each other's sin upon itself as Jesus did.

When a community wishes to express what it wants for itself as a totality, it usually does so through some mechanism whereby that totality gets stated as best it can. Officials in a community are the ordinary way in which this is done. They *say* the community by their very office. But what are the officials in the sacrament of penance *saying?* Ideally, they are the expression of the whole community's commitment to forgiveness. They are the pledge of the whole community's acceptance of the sinner. They are acting as individuals, but they want to say more. If the sinner can pick this "more" up, if he can break out of the frame of mind which concentrates on God's forgiveness alone, if he can see the community in its official, he will have a glimmer of that communal acceptance that Christ promises.

Can the doubt whether the community is actually committed to forgiving ever be overcome? Can the bond between the community official and the community itself ever be taken seriously? May not the official himself fail in communicating a forgiveness that others in the community would better provide? Our poverty is evident here, and our suspicion. But the sacrament of penance remains the symbol of and a demand upon the community's commitment to be forgivers. In the hope of this truth, sinners might find that *room to say out loud themselves* that they so much desire.

II. THE GROUP EVENT

Our overall task is to study how our being in a group
influences what eventually gets said about God,
Jesus, sacraments, or, in this case,
the sacrament of penance.

To this end the group is to select
one of its members to be its minister
of this sacrament, with the proviso that it first
shares the responsibility of explaining
to the candidate what is thereby involved.

From the beginning of the session, there was confusion in the group concerning the candidate. One member, Judy, consistently supposed that the candidate was the one who would **lead the group's discussion,** "asking questions and getting responses." Though that language fits what confessors sometimes do in the sacrament, it was clear that Judy was concerned about the procedures to be followed by the group to insure a fruitful discussion. Everyone else understood the candidate to mean the potential **minister of the sacrament.** They remained somewhat puzzled by Judy's remarks, although no one ever stopped her to ask what might be going on. In fact, at the outset some thought she meant by her candidate the **recipient** of the sacrament. This reaction (shared by the facilitator) showed an initial preoccupation with the role of penitent. *Fantasies of self-revelation and exposure were near the surface,* and one member actually raised the possibility of his making a confession early in the session.

Secondly, there was frequent reference in the early part of the session to there being "nine members" in the group. Actually there were ten, if you included the facilitator. Even after the facilitator challenged the count, so to speak, the group kept speaking about its "nine members." *This seemed like some kind of declaration of independence vis à vis the facilitator. But it also made the group*

60

wonder whether the same exclusion might happen to it individually, that is, whether someone would be left out if he or she showed any leadership.

Harriet was the first to question, "whether we need to confess to a representative of the Church." This established the issue of the nature of the minister of the sacrament, and the group would be working with this issue steadily. Sides were quickly drawn. Phil, Ed, Harriet, and Judy (if we can count her as talking to the theological issue) clearly were in favor of **everyone** being the minister. Celia, John, Cathy, Alice, and Steve expressed themselves as seeing value in there being **one** minister. Even in the latter camp, the minister was described gingerly, as though no one wanted to attribute anything to him that would discriminate against those who were not the minister. For example, Cathy called the minister, "just a representative for us who already are ministers of the sacrament." John agreed that the one who "officially represents us doesn't shut the rest of us out." John also related the need for the minister to the size of the community; he admitted that having one official minister of the sacrament added to his sense of security. Celia's defense of the one minister rested on tradition: we are supposed to have one. Steve saw the value of one minister as having someone, "to call the people together, to call them to a sense of sharing, to stir them up to a sense of their sinfulness."

The facilitator insisted, during all of this, that ten people not nine were working on the task. This might seem like a distraction from the group's work on the question of one vs. many ministers of the sacrament. In point of fact, it was intended to focus the group on why it might be having trouble breaking the rigid either/or it had given itself. *The reason for its impasse was that the group was "excluding" each other by not reacting to each other in more than a perfunctory way.* The facilitator's interventions finally brought from Cathy the admission that the group was indeed influencing each other in what was getting said about the minister. She felt the influence was negative. Phil concurred, saying that he was being influenced negatively by the "little sheet" on which was written the task designed by the facilitator. On the surface, these two remarks came out of nowhere, the facilitator in no way spelling out the foregoing argument himself. *But they show that the group was quite aware they were hardly interacting on the issue, or, where they did interact, it was only to contradict one another without confronting one another. So everyone felt particularly isolated (like the tenth member) at this point,* and Phil and Cathy were conveying the group's sense of isolation. This brought the following response.

Judy: Is there even a value to being in community? Steve mentioned that the function of the minister is to call people together. What benefit is there in being called together as a community? It's a lot easier to live by yourself.

Ed challenged this view. He had earlier been himself challenged by Judy for raising questions "out there" rather than questions that touched him. He now countered:

Ed: To my mind, the sacrament centers on community, on relationships. It means to foster and deepen relationships. I don't think they are ever totally broken, but they can become very frail. Jesus wanted to make us realize that we could need one another, to the incredible degree that we could not survive without each other. I disagree with what Judy said, that it's much harder to live alone.

Judy: Easier.

Ed: It isn't easier. It's much more terrible to live alone. In some ways it's harder to live in community, but at least you have someone there to relate to. But if you are strictly by yourself, you have no one to relate to. So I think the sacrament has to do with deepening relationships, bringing people closer to one another for the sake of the needs we have, for assistance.

This started the group off on a discussion of the best language to describe what the community does for the sinner. Reconciliation and healing were offered as developments of Ed's thought. Steve remarked that Jesus' healings were all very close personal encounters in which he usually touched the person first. Ed would not accept these developments. He saw the role of the community only as reinforcing the fact that we have already healed ourselves. "I think," he said, "we've put too much responsibility on Jesus or on God. I think it's our responsibility both to heal ourselves and to encourage others to heal themselves."

John tried to salvage the view that the minister had some role besides reinforcing what the sinner was doing for himself. He made a case for the need of active forgiving on the part of the Christian, any Christian. *No one at this point was about to tell Ed that they thought he was wrong. Instead, Judy took the group off in another direction.* She suggested that they consider the things for which someone might need forgiveness. "You mean, what sin is?" asked Ed.

As soon as this issue was raised, the group *accelerated the demands* on the minister. He had to be from a select group (Celia). It had to be someone with whom one could be comfortable (Judy). He could not put his personal code on the penitent (Thea). The facilitator asked whether a comfortable person could be found in **this** group, whereupon *the tone of the group became silent and labored.* There was murmured admission that they were indeed overloading the role of the minister:

> *Harriet:* I feel very convinced that we all have the ability to forgive each other. Then on the other hand I feel that some people are more sensitive. There are people with certain gifts.
>
> *Ed:* Maybe we all feel that everyone can forgive, but at the same time we don't believe that they really do forgive.
>
> *Judy:* Or if they really care.
>
> *Ed:* Because they're total strangers to us, or we really don't know if they will forgive us.
>
> *Phil:* Are we really looking for forgiveness, or are we looking primarily or equally for counselling at the same time? That's why we seek out sensitive people.

These four speakers were paradoxically the original proponents of "many" ministers of the sacrament rather than "one" minister. They now were the spokesman for a certain sense of impossibility, of community frustration. They were loath to attribute to the minister "certain gifts" but they were even more sceptical about the community at large. The next phase was all the more interesting for that reason. Phil launched off on why, without rejecting the sacrament, and even in the midst of it, he did not want to get involved **at all** with the minister's forgiveness. He preferred to tell his sin to God, without "taking on the minister's humanity." Ed thought Phil was agreeing with his own theory, that we forgive and heal ourselves. But Phil rejected this, saying mysteriously that God's forgiveness is important because, "God is anxious to keep his creation going."

The group next fell into a kind of moody pensiveness. The speakers could hardly be heard. The few words that floated free were words like "loving," "consoling," "transparent." The facilitator asked if the group was loving each other at such a great pace in order to avoid selecting a candidate. This brought the group back to where it was before, to the qualifications of the minister, with one difference. Alice insisted that the minister both represented forgiveness and exemplified it. Ed returned his favorite thesis, that the minister reminds us we have forgiven ourselves. *The difference lay in that the group began, for the first time, to express disagreement with and to each other.* Celia told Alice that she was asking too much with her second requirement. Alice told Ed she disagreed with him. *But this very boldness seemed to frighten the group. It kept avoiding the possibility that there was a candidate for minister in its own midst.* When pressed by the facilitator on this score, it very laboriously came up with a candidate, John, who seemed to be the natural leader of the group, thus far, in staying on the task.

With John as candidate, the group then reviewed the requirements for the job of minister, mixing those previously mentioned (comforting, stirring up, forgiving) with some new ones (opening the sinner up by means of communication techniques). John's worry about his future post was with "knowing what was sin or not." How could he be the minister if he did not know what sin was? Alice tried to ease his dilemma, encouraging him to forgive people at the level where they are. "I don't think it would matter whether it was a sin or not," she said. Ed, on the other hand, demanded great preparation for the job from John, special training, dedication, and a certain life-style. *The group session ended with John's consternation growing.*

III. THEOLOGICAL IMPLICATIONS

Throughout this session statements about the sacrament of penance were constantly masking what are in large part statements about the group-life. This makes it very difficult to know whether to take the group's statements about the sacrament at face value. For example, the terms "facilitator" and "confessor" are actually used synonymously. The group does "other business" while it talks theology. Sometimes we are alerted to the presence of these two levels of activity in groups by the tone of the group: sad and languid, hostile and disjointed, giddy and frenzied. Sometimes gestures and looks accompany what is being said which indicates that an argument is in progress beneath the surface. Sometimes remarks are directed to one person when it is clear they are intended for another. This roundabout shuttling of messages across the group can, it is true, add up to a continuation of the solid theological work of the group. But it can also be a distraction from that work. It can mean that people are primarily engaged in face-saving, getting even, joining sides, asking pardon, unruffling feathers, inviting sympathy, or simply hell-raising.

If we examine the sacrament-of-penance group for these levels of activity, we find three clear instances of it. First, Phil is sceptical about getting forgiveness from anyone but God. He makes central to his understanding of the sacrament the fact that it has to do with God. Yet, he positively resists distinctions within the group. No one should have more responsibility to be forgiving than anyone else. Theoretically, it should not matter to Phil what anyone "down here" is doing, since his statements about the sacrament effectively remove it from "down here." So it seems that Phil, in describing God's role in the sacrament, is also making a strong statement about his lack of confidence *in the group*.

Second, Ed insists that sinners forgive themselves, and this is proposed as important for the description of the sacrament. A minister (or anyone else for that matter) does nothing more than ratify what the sinner has already done for himself. On the other hand, Ed insists that the "ratifier" have tremendous qualifications and training. Moreover, Ed is the one who makes the case for "needing others," and the language he uses for relationships with others is most tactile, warm and tender. How put this together with his kind of ruggedly individualistic self-healing by the sinner? So it seems that Ed, besides talking to the issue of the sacrament, is exhorting *the group* in its behavior to be both kind and independently resourceful.

Third, the closer the group got to talking about a minister of the sacrament, the more it became aware of the community whose minister the candidate would be. Part of this awareness of community consisted of a desire that the community be *loving* and *forgiving* in the sacrament. Part of it consisted of worrying whether the community *could ever agree* on just what sin was. Partly, the community was seen to need stirring up to see the *presence of sin* in its midst. The minister of the sacrament was supposed to satisfy all these qualities that the community needed. These cautions, however, while they are set down for the minister of the *sacrament,* serve as well to sum up what each member of the group was saying to every other member about the *group-life* itself.

Looking at the theological language of the group, then, we suffer a kind of double vision. It is terribly difficult to sort out the theology from the "other business" of the group. How then do we evaluate the theological end product? When seen against the background of the group-experience, it looks as though the theological language in the group is a matter of the survival of the fittest. Truth seems to yield to persuasiveness, and persuasiveness seems to rely on very feeble, even shady, criteria.

We certainly do not want to say that, simply because the group interaction is influencing the members, the theology they present cannot contain their serious convictions and reflections on the religious topic at hand. On the other hand, what a person says in a group does not merely reflect his view of "human nature in general." Individuals do have such views, and these views do affect us as we theologize. But in a group these same views are played out against the reality of a concrete group of "human natures." We are forced to test our individual theories about "man" against the reality of these men and women present here. An individual's attitude towards "people" cannot remain abstract in the presence of *these* people. The group setting influences what gets said theologically partly because, in an immediate and sensible way, it challenges our presuppositions about human nature, the very ones which have influenced our views of God or of Jesus.

But there is more. We are better able to read theological suggestions for what they are when we view them against this background of group-life. There is a tendency to consider the theological formulations of a group or religious body as placidly objective reflections on religious experience, capturing that experience the way a camera catches a scene with permanence and fidelity. It is foreign to our habits to see theology as the fruit of competition, of an unwillingness to face certain aspects of our reality, of an intellectual aridity and blanking-out because of the strong emotional issues involved, of the fear of contradicting, of an impatience with other views, of ambition or even of revenge, of power, or of subservience. None of these things in themselves argues to the truth or falsehood of a particular theological stance. The question is: can the observation, tracking and analysis of their origins in group-life push us to ask further questions about theological statements that might open up those statements to further development, nuances, compromise, and illustration? We are talking here about the enrichment of the theology, and not about any magic route to the "right" theology. Very often the group setting seems to create a chamber of alternating noises and silences, starts and stops, marking of time and tentative movement in one or another direction. It is from this complicated experience that we can learn both the need to take the theological topic further and the direction we might profitably take it in.

An example of this process can be seen in the penance group. The talk in the group about relationships, closeness, assistance and mutual need was kept so broad and general as to be exasperating. They offered no idea of how the closeness that accompanies *forgiving* differs from other obvious forms of closeness that have nothing to do with sin and forgiveness. So much so that the group seemed to want to forgive each other for being alive. Comparatively little time was spent by the group on describing what forgiving looks like, why people need it or need to do it, and how it could be illustrated from experience.

* * * * *

Yet, several strains that *were* sounded by the group do offer a fruitful starting place for this theological question about forgiveness. A picture of forgiveness can be assembled from the preoccupations of the group: people are anxious not to be thought less of, not to be judged—both fair descriptions of forgiving. Also, forgiving had something to do with clarifying for a person the dimensions of his misbehavior, of throwing light on the dark areas of the self, not in the sense of microscopically isolating an evil spot, but in the sense of juxtaposing moral failure with the goodness and potential for growth in a person. There was, finally, the image of forgiving as taking on the humanity of the sinner. These considerations begin to provide a *content* to forgiveness which pins it down and makes more clear what the responsibility of the minister in this sacrament might be.

A second contribution that the observation of the group might make to the theology of the sacrament would come from considering the fate of God in the penance group. God was strangely absent from the deliberations. This could mean that the group simply was not making an issue of God where they thought he was not all that involved. But were they all peacefully convinced that God never thinks less of people despite their sins? Or was the judgment of God such an ominous mystery that it was not even broached? At any rate, the more the group reflected on its own internal complications, and on the issues of forgiving with which it was wrestling, the more God became a conscious factor. ''God got us into this mess in the first place,'' said one member. The group stimulates by its very experience the realization that God gives to men, or lets occur, a kind of relentless responsibility to act for themselves. There is no *deus ex machina*, no magic, no possibility of a dependence which robs us of our independence.

The issue of competence is raised by the group in crescendo fashion. How competent does one need to be to be the minister of this sacrament? How competent does one need to be to assume one's role in the group? How can we be competent if the priest is the only competent one? The facilitator is automatically recognized as competent (however true this may be). This extends both to his being teacher (competent in sacramental theology), and to his ''running'' the group (competent to behave in a group ''as one should''). Needless to say, his competence is not as much an issue as the group makes it, since all in the group have the right and responsibility to use their competence for the task. Yet, much of the group's energy is expended to discover and find room for the competences in its midst, both theologically and for the life of the group. In this effort, and as an expression of it, the ''competent'' facilitator is both excluded (by the nine) and relied upon (by pausing to reflect on each of his interventions and remarks—which they do for each other only, alas, after emotional outbursts).

Out of all this, the question of God's competence and of God's relationship to our competence comes vividly home. We are given a share in the divine life where energetic forgiving is the normal thing. It is God's graciousness to us and confidence in us that is to make us competent forgivers. But do we believe that?

V

The
eucharist
group

N I. BACKGROUND*

owhere more than in the matter of the Eucharist are central issues of
the Christian faith engaged. By this is not meant the issue of Jesus' real
presence, although that too must be considered. But it can be a kind
of hide-and-seek diversion from other equally important topics:
What *kind* of Jesus is present? What is Jesus present *for?* How does
his presence allow the presence of others? Is the community "really
present"? With what expected comportment and sensibilities? What
are the distinctive roles of Jesus and of his faithful in this eucharistic
celebration?

Even the term "celebration" calls for some scrutiny. All that is
denoted by "eucharist" is "thanksgiving." But not every thanksgiving is the cause for celebration. Sometimes a thanksgiving is
dutiful, or filled with sentiments of relief and emerging calm; sometimes it is casual or full of purpose. Those thanksgivings which we
do celebrate often concern the fact that *our* skins have been saved. It
remains to be seen whether or not the Christian Eucharist is meant to
emphasize that narrow and egoistic perspective.

The history of the theology of the Eucharist reflects a certain
tension that rarely has been resolved. We might say that these
theologies tend toward one of two poles: at the first pole the Eucharist
is clearly devotional, centered on Jesus, preoccupied with his
personal fate, reenacting his drama, concentrating on the partic-
ipant's union with him by means of the ritual communion. At the
other pole the Eucharist is meal and fellowship, fostering a horizontal

*See p. 10.

69

unity among his followers, eliciting their camaraderie and combined service. So the question comes down to: who is celebrating what and with whom at a Eucharist?

An example of this polar tension can be seen even in the work of noted biblical scholars. A comparison of Willi Marxsen and Joachim Jeremias will bear this out.[1]

Marxsen attempts to understand the Eucharist against the background of his overall understanding of Jesus. The latter may be summed up as follows:[2]

A. Jesus did not call for faith in himself.

B. Rather, he put men before God and brought them to a realization that God was anticipating their final state of friendship with him now.

C. Jesus demonstrated this by what he did, e.g., by eating with sinners, healing, and the like—all traditional signs of behavior consistent with God's final Kingdom.

D. It is he, Jesus, who does all this, but not much is made of this fact by him.

E. At Easter, that is, when Jesus is no longer physically present, a special problem arises for his disciples:
   1. They wish to continue living the new life of God's eschatological presence.
   2. But they wish this not simply in some doctrinaire fashion, i.e., not as a theoretical possibility for human living.
   3. The conviction was too strong among them that it was Jesus who inaugurated their way of life (cf. D. above), and they wanted to express the perduring influence of him on their lives.

F. They began to seek ways of expressing his centrality to the eschatological message. So that whereas before, what matters is Jesus, his quality, his being, or his place in relation to God, now, after Easter, his person is interpreted in ways that will highlight the uniqueness of his function. It will now be stressed that *his* actions were the start of the eschatological way of living and so exert a perduring influence even now.

Against this background Marxsen studies the New Testament tradition concerning the Lord's Supper. He argues that Jesus practiced a kind of fellowship meal, whose main function was to indicate the presence of God's final Kingdom among men. It was this kind of fellowship experience that would be the normal practice of the earliest Christians.

Marxsen maintains that there was no one famous Last Supper at which the historical Jesus underwent some kind of personal crisis and expressed that crisis in the language of a new passover. Rather, the New Testament descriptions of *a* Last Supper are reconstructions, legitimate reconstructions, with the following aim: to preserve the memory of Jesus' original inspiration and his perduring influence on their observance of fellowship meals. For, according to Marxsen, they were convinced that, with Jesus, *God* is perduringly committed to bring his Kingdom among men. In this sense, the reality of the new age is always given "through Jesus."

How best express this conviction? The Jewish contemporaries of Jesus could easily grasp the message of their relationship with God, and with each other in God, through the image of fellowship-meal, where camaraderie and unity would be stressed. And Jesus' inspiration for these meals would have been obvious. But once Jesus is gone and the mission of preaching the eschatological good news to the gentiles begins, new ways of expressing these same things must be sought. The old ways would not impress someone fresh from Hellenistic paganism, whose thought-patterns required images much more tied to physical phenomena. Hence God and Jesus would *have* to be thought of as physically present in the meal, literally, as it were, bringing to pass the eschatological reality of familiar personal relationship with God. The presence of God-in-Jesus was located now *in* the bread and wine. Gradually the sense of meal-fellowship was lost and a "Mass" emerged, in which communing with God-in-Jesus was understood in a literal sense.

Marxsen claims some textual foundation for his view. He notes a progression in the New Testament tradition on "the Last Supper" from one level to the next:

1. At the earliest stage, in the meals described in Acts 2 and 4 (texts referring to a period much earlier than the date of Acts' actual composition), there is little indication that Christians were practicing the full-blown Eucharists of the synoptic writers.

2. At a second stage (which Paul cites in 1 Cor. 11:23-26 as an earlier tradition), whatever meaning attaches to the bread and wine, it is not, according to Marxsen, one which has the community eating and drinking the body and blood of Jesus. The earlier tradition, he says, does not even concentrate on the fact that the bread and wine are being distributed to be eaten and drunk.[3] Rather, the communitarian aspect of the meal is being underscored. Strong

reference is made to the "cup of the covenant" and to "the body" of the community. True, this fellowship and solidarity have their basis in the death (blood) of Jesus, but no connection with the bread or wine is thereby implied.

3. At a third stage, represented in Paul's editorial commentary on the tradition he is citing, we find for the first time reference to the cultic eating and drinking of the bread and wine. The normal meal setting has, by this time, been moved up to just before the cultic meal. Paul has no objection to this. But even here, says Marxsen, Paul is not saying that the bread and wine are *elements containing* Jesus in some sense. He wants instead to stress the *sharing* that is appropriate to the Eucharist.[4] The Corinthians are not sharing the cultic bread and wine and hence are violating Jesus' kind of fellowship.[5] But in order to make his point with them, Paul has to use *their* language. They were quite familiar with the debate raging at that time about whether it was *legitimate* or not to *eat* food which had been sacrificed to idols and then sold in the marketplace for common consumption. Paul makes reference to this kind of thinking when he asks whether Christians can *legitimately eat* the cultic meal if they were at the same time violating fellowship. His problem with their "eating" goes only this far. He does not speak of the bread and wine as sacred elements, even though a Hellenistic mentality might think that the reason for legitimacy-illegitimacy lies *in* the food itself.[6]

4. At a fourth stage, in Mark's institution account, for example, an emphasis on sacred elements of bread and wine is presupposed and accepted. The Hellenistic cultural mentality mentioned earlier has apparently won out. The Church discovers that, by cooperating with a mentality which calls for "goodness" and "badness" to be *in* foods, it can also provide for the need to highlight Jesus' role in first bringing the eschatological message and his perduring influence, under God, in the sustaining of that message. We arrive, therefore, at a rite in which sacred bread and wine are the focus of the eucharistic celebration, are literally Jesus. Jesus' place is now guaranteed. If the original emphasis on community fellowship fades it will not at least be totally lost.

* * * * *

It is clear that Marxsen is arguing for the real presence of the eschatological community rather than for the real presence of Jesus in the elements of bread and wine. Our point is not to dwell on the difficulties with this way of thinking. Marxsen's thinking on the Last Supper follows logically enough from his general principles of christology. The weakest of these is Marxsen's attributing to "Jesus" what seems in fact to be what God is doing or what we are doing. The present state, the present personal activity and functioning of the once historical Jesus is left hazy in the extreme. God seems to be acting now "in Jesus" for old time's sake, or for purposes best known to himself. If, as Marxsen implies, the ritual meal of Mark's Gospel has already lost the sense of fraternal fellowship that Jesus had given it, then the christological "developments" which led to that result were not developments but betrayals. Nor would there have been any further reason for Jesus' eucharistic presence to be preached, since people would begin to wonder *what* Jesus was influencing in such a perduring manner if a basic sense of community had not survived. That the primitive community could have bollixed up things so quickly is unlikely. Even less likely is the acceptance by the Palestinian mother churches of such radical adaptation to the supposed Hellenist mentality. But these are christological arguments that belong elsewhere. We will let Jeremias present the scriptural data on the Eucharist from, as it were, the other pole.

* * * * *

In a much more traditional vein, Jeremias argues to the historicity of one *(the)* Last Supper,[7] and to the essential continuity between the stages of the New Testament tradition. The critical aspects of that last meal stand out: first, Jeremias maintains that Jesus signaled the importance of the meal by personally fasting at it.[8] Second, Jesus performs the traditional role of the host at a Passover meal by selectively interpreting the elements of the meal.[9] While Jesus singles out the bread and the wine for interpretation, he closely associates these with the slaughtered paschal lamb, stressing the brokenness of the bread and the bloodlike quality of the wine. Moreover, he conveys to those present that these elements express his own plight of the moment, faced with the prospect of being literally broken and bloodied by his enemies.

Third, Jesus expresses the realization that his predicament is essentially expiatory.[10] By this is meant that Jesus has an acute sense that fidelity to this moment of his life—the moment when he is most threatened for the way he lives, for all the things he stands for —is crucial. It will affect others in ways that are probably not clear to him, but *that* it will affect others he is certainly conscious. In Jesus' case, the awareness is apparently colored by second thoughts about whether his followers are worth the effort. He also seems to realize vividly that it is his own loving Father in heaven who has somehow brought him to this point. Jesus' sense of the expiatory quality of the moment, then, comprises a challenge to his deepest identity: he, the man of large-scale community vision, finds himself dependent on the violence or weakness of others, depended upon by his friends who share his vision, dependent on the Father and depended upon by the Father in the whole dizzying situation. This is what it is to expiate. We should not think that Jesus' expiating loses its human shape and character. Every person's critical choices are expiatory in the same sense as those of Jesus. We have only to recall those moments of our own lives when we have discovered our identity to be linked to other people with whom God has gotten us involved.

Perhaps this is why Jeremias considers the fourth noteworthy aspect of the Last Supper to be Jesus' request to those present to pray for him.[11] This requires shifting the traditional translation to read, "Do this so that God may remember me" (1 Cor. 11:24). But even apart from this interpretation of a particular text, there is plentiful evidence in the various accounts that Jesus was distraught. Fifth, Jeremias explains that Jesus' *giving* the bread and wine to his table-companions is significant.[12] It has the effect of including them in what is transpiring at table and promising them a share in it.

But a share in what? If Jesus were only offering them a share in his worries, in the brokenness of the lamb, it would be an even bleaker evening than it seems to have been. Jeremias is not complete at this point. We must suppose that later, at the distribution of the bread, the *thrust* of Jesus' earlier commentary (*haggadah*) on the meal shifted somewhat. What had earlier been broken and bloody (or so the bread and wine, in its association with the slain lamb, had seemed to Jesus) becomes in the course of the meal what it really is—food and drink, sustenance and refreshment, shared gift. For this to be the case, Jesus must have come to some resolution during the meal, in the direction of accepting his fate and circumstances. The bread and wine thus signify him in an entirely new sense. They become signs of his worth, his identity as God's man, his being for others in an expiatory way, of the legitimacy of his program, of the wrongheadedness of his enemies—all the issues which in fact fed the crisis of that meal.

Quite clearly, the Last Supper in Jeremias' reconstruction (and with the further comments we have offered) is the drama of Jesus first. The table-fellowship takes its character, tone and structure from him.

* * * * *

The issue between Marxsen and Jeremias, however, is only superficially one of historical evidences for or against a Last Supper. We suggest that more basic questions lie at the bottom of the matter. Marxsen feels one of these strongly, and considers it to be the chief preoccupation of the post-Easter Church: how do you celebrate Jesus' fellowship when he is not around? Does not his absence mean that we are to turn to each other and to God, and was not this his purpose all along in his earthly life? On the other hand, Marxsen seems to accuse the post-Easter Church of a failure of nerve, of not being able to sustain the eschatological experience without inventing a lot of quasi-historical incidents about Jesus, of not simply believing that, though God began the eschaton in Jesus, he can without difficulty continue it without any physical presence of Jesus in the Church. But is this the only kind of failure of nerve?

Jeremias, on the other hand, seems so locked into the final drama of Jesus that he fails to show how community fellowship is related to it. He agrees that table-fellowship is a sacral element of the meal. But is he sufficiently sensitive to the need of showing how the community can be assembled around an event which is, at the same time, so personal to Jesus and so crucial to them?

The problem is that table-fellowship throws Christians together with many unresolved interrelationships among them, even apart from the quality of their relationships with God and with Jesus. If we consult the predispositions of people for celebrations of *any* kind, we uncover dimensions which ultimately influence our reactions to the Eucharist. People have expectations, hesitations, even demands about celebrations: Will I enjoy myself? Is it a special occasion? Will I meet people who are interesting? Will I be entertained (passively)? What shall I wear? What should I bring? How will I conduct myself? Will children be there? Will women be there? Will men? Do I have to talk to so-and-so? How long will it last? Can I go and still get all my work done? Will I have to clean up? What is in it for *them?* Is this a social requirement? Is it planned or spontaneous? Will I be outclassed financially or educationally? Will it be one of those good old days things? Will it be job talk or gripe session? Do I have to be on my best behavior there? Will my shadowy past be known? Will the talk center on the food? Can I just be, or need I analyze it? Will it bind me afterwards to any commitments?

All these factors influence the way people approach celebrations. Do they not also influence our approach to the Eucharist? To assume too quickly that we can gather together under these circumstances with proper attention to and measured appreciation of Jesus' drama is very sanguine. There is enough complexity to the issues contained in the Eucharist to make us wonder: do we make it Jesus' event simply because it is too hard to make it ours? Is devotion to Jesus being used to escape our disillusionment with community? Or is the search for community distracting us from the person of Jesus? Probably, the truth of the Eucharist should be for us what it was for Jesus, including *all* the complexities, honoring *all* the reality, relating *all* the persons involved.

II. THE GROUP EVENT

Our overall task is to study how our being in a group influences what gets said about God, Jesus, the sacraments, or, especially in this case, the sacrament of the eucharist. To this end the group is to share responsibility for constructing a eucharistic liturgy, explaining as they do so how individual suggestions are appropriate or not to the eucharist.

At Frances' suggestion, the group brainstorms in order to find out what each member thinks of the Eucharist. Sharing, thanksgiving, celebration, forgiving, openness to the Father, word-and-meal, unanimity, healing, are all offered as descriptions of the Eucharist. Kathy asks whether these descriptions should be accepted without further ado, or whether any criteria should guide their acceptance or rejection. *As a challenge to Frances' leadership, and in order to avoid the painful implications of Kathy's question, a shift in direction occurs:* "The group should start with how **it** feels rather than with defining things, which would be too much like a class" (Bob); "The group should start with where **we** are" (Mary); a common understanding of the Eucharist will "automatically" emerge (Bob and Mary). From this new perspective, Bob and Mary define liturgy as a matter of "listening and responding."

The pain of one rejected member continues without being handled: (drily) "So we have mutual agreement" (Frances). *The group is not facing the tense shift that has occured.* While "listening and responding" could be a business-like description of the Eucharist, *it also reflects the group's awareness of its own problem of listening and responding.* So the facilitator asks, "Is the group warning each other through this language of listening, that is, is it saying to each other, "You had better listen"? *Another member takes issue with the previous failure to respond to her:* "Is the group—for example, the two of you, Bob and Mary—warning some of us that there are certain things it does not want to hear?" (Kathy).

After a desultory protest about its general innocence, the group further analyzes "listening and responding" as a description of the

Eucharist: they may be verbal or silent; they involve a communication with God and with others; they are subject to distractions which stem from the rigid formalism of fixed readings, standard canons, and so on (Mary and Doris). Bob asks how such a description is proper to **eucharistic** liturgical prayer. Does it not also and equally fit **any** group-prayer? *A rosy hue descends upon the group:* "If only liturgy could have the kind of open communication that we have in this group, where we know each other and do not feel alone."

Bob's question has gone unanswered. The self-description of the group at this point is patently untrue. Some are alone, and communication is hardly open. The group has already intimated (intimidated?) that some members want no "fixed canons" in the discussion of liturgy. Not everyone agrees to this, but the topic is being avoided. So the facilitator comments, "The group seems to be undecided as to whether it **is** happy in its communication. Perhaps it sees a parallel between the presence of a canon in the liturgy and the presence of a fixed written text of the task here in the group."

To face its fixed task, the group must return to Bob's question. It admits a difference between the liturgy and other kinds of group prayer. In the former, the use of certain texts is required (Sandra). This requirement seems to clash with what is more meaningful (Doris), and yet it cannot be dispensed with since it is God-given (Mary). In these remarks, *the group is trying to discover who in it* **is** *fixed in the matter of required texts in the liturgy.* Bob outlines certain "essential elements" that belong in all liturgy:

1. the word of God

2. the prayer of thanksgiving
   a) invocation of the Spirit
   b) words of institution
   c) linking what we are doing to Jesus' dying and rising

3. communion.

Mike interrupts to express the fear that the group has dismissed too lightly the facilitator's last intervention. *Actually, the group seems quite clear that the facilitator is not talking about his own fixed position but about theirs. Mike's concern for the facilitator seems rather to stem partly from his apprehension about defending a fairly fixed position of his own (which he soon does), and partly from his frustration with the indirection that characterizes communication in the group at this point. If Mary and Doris are opponents of "the canon," why can they not be confronted directly?*

While Bob sees a certain "tyranny of the text" both in the liturgy and in "what we are doing here," he does not think that this inevitably impedes our creativity. Nor need we say that the essential elements of the liturgy are "given to us by God." For, they are, and **were** in their original Last Supper setting, instances of **human** listening and responding.

The group is beginning to struggle with the legitimacy and scope of creativity in its midst, both in the matter of drawing up a liturgy and in the matter of living the group-life. The obvious creative leadership of Bob gets no response and seems, if anything, to depress the group. So the facilitator asks, "Is there anything more to doing the task than listening and responding?" *The group takes this as a rebuke. It expresses guilt at not having listened or responded earlier. And it expresses hurt at not having been responded to* (Frances). The facilitator interjects, "The point was to arouse neither guilt nor resentment, but to examine what contributes to the theological task." *More guilt is expressed:* "We're not getting down to action" (Sandra); "We're not ritualizing what is communicated" (Frances). Bob and Mary return to the theological work: "Besides listening and responding, creativity is required for the task." But there is no response.

The group, as Frances has just hinted, is now faced with the pain of creativity in a group. [To do the task, the group must, in a sense, canonize (Frances' ritualize) each other's creativity.] *This they are finding hard to do, since some have already said what they thought about "fixed canons."* The facilitator tries to get the group to face the negative aspect of creativity, so as to transcend it. He remarks, "Each time (twice) the group cites the text of the task, it leaves out the part which reads "explaining. . .how individual suggestions are appropriate **or not** to the Eucharist."

The group turns to lamenting its fate, cementing its position, yet trying to free itself. Its question at this point is how to be creative in the face of liturgical laws: "Authorities know more than I do" (Sandra); "Liturgy is not our property" (Mike); "Liturgy is not an expression of people" (Frances); "I want to know if it is valid, i.e., changing bread into the body of Jesus" (Sandra); "How can we talk of structures when we're dealing with persons?" (Frances); "I'll make suggestions for a liturgy, but I won't act on them. Or I'll even act on them, but not officially" (Mike).

The group has projected an external obstacle to its creativity, Rome's laws. Bob alone feels that his creativity can work in the framework of tradition. *But there are more than external obstacles to be dealt with.* So the facilitator asks, "Is rejection by Rome the

only problem for this group? Is there no rejection going on here?''
This intervention brings a twofold reaction:

(1) How can we be creative in the face of other people's rejection? "Do we as a group accept in principle that all suggestions about the liturgy will be appropriate?" (Kathy);
"Rome is in here, too" (Mike);

(2) What *criteria* govern the rejection of anyone's suggestions?
This brings the group back to Kathy's original question:
"Only meaningful suggestions are acceptable" (Mary);
"We should not simply be giving our personal views, but
should be working for the benefit of the group" (Mary);
"Agreement kills creativity" (Mary); "Where there is
union, there is celebration" (Doris); "How can there be
eucharistic unity where there is so much diversity?"

III. THEOLOGICAL IMPLICATIONS

It would seem at first glance that the Eucharist group offered little in
the way of theological content for a picture of the sacrament. Even
granting the limitations of time, the theological work performed was
rather scant. Listening, responding, fixed texts, Jesus' words, invoca-
tions, thanksgiving, communing, unity within plurality—all these
present us with a somewhat disjointed picture of the Eucharist. Not
that these descriptions are inaccurate in capturing some of the most
common sentiments and experiences related to the Eucharist that one
meets in the Church today. In fact, they mirror the glorious jumble of
things that afflict and uplift the normal community of Christians at
their eucharistic celebrations. In this sense they are richly true to the
felt experience of many who approach the most solemn mystery of
Jesus. But as articulate, measured, and illuminating syntheses they
fail considerably.

A second look at the group, however, reveals a magnificent irony.
Without entering in detail into individual performances it became
vividly clear that theological creativity was present in the Eucharist
group to the extent that those who were trying to create the liturgy
were "present to themselves in the group." That is to say, the
attempt to "give" theologically succeeded or failed as the group
members identified themselves, achieved a degree of self-possession
and resolve in the group. This enabled them not simply to survive in
the emotional swirl of the group, but to push ahead to do the theological work of the group.

Decisions to accept their position in the group, to neutralize and
channel the forces at work on them from beyond the group, to be

themselves in all their talent and responsibility, were put to individuals throughout the session. Each person suffered certain fantasies about the group, about how they got there and whether their coming was worthwhile, about the reception their actions would get from others, about the profit others might have from their generous efforts, about the reasonableness and utility of the whole scene. Listening was difficult, and responding more so. Allegiances shifted treacherously, enemies were unmasked as friends. The creative person seemed endowed with some capacity to do what had to be done despite the flux and conflicting movements in the room. How these developments parallel the Last Supper experience can be seen with a little reflection.

This struggle seems to demand the special struggle of a few in the group, or even of one. The group must *see someone do it*. The vision of another person's confrontation with the dynamic of the group in pursuit of the task is a lesson to all. For they experience that, in such a leader's struggle, death (pain, humiliation, fear, depression, paralysis) is not really death, but rather it gives rise to progress in the work of the group. Those who identify themselves honestly in terms of where the group is become the remarkable figures in the group. While the savior-of-the-group role can be overdone, it is undeniable that seeing the process of death-resurrection in one individual's contribution to the group is the trigger for others in the group to assess their own potential contribution. The pain and passion of one individual in the group have an obvious impact, though not always a successful one, on the benefits accruing to the group at large. Through it the group has final cause for celebration.

Symbolisms change, too, in the course of the session. Taking its own language as the basic symbol used by the group, that language (e.g., listening, canon, create, respond, commune, essentials) passes through a purification process. Pain, bitterness, fear, aggression, suspicion, innuendo, all echo from beneath the surface meaning of the "theological" suggestions made in the group, influencing the very choice of words, the grammar, the inflections, the sequence, the imagery, the whole skein of understanding that is emerging. As it is purified in a developing climate of trust, of fidelity to the work of the task, of creative initiatives, the *same* language then seems to function in its own right as resource for the theological task, operating now fully and directly for what it is. The words which carried an ambiguous and unresolved meaning during part of the session are transformed, in the course of it, into positive contributions to the theological work.

What we have been describing thus far occurs in all groups. What is so special about its occurrence here? Nothing, except the irony.

The irony lies in the fact that, as the Eucharist group seemingly flounders in its task of describing Jesus' Eucharist, its own dynamics are so strikingly parallel to the dynamics of the Last Supper as we described them in the first section of this chapter. Our first reaction to this group was that it added nothing, reinforced nothing, and said nothing to the author's theological presuppositions. The parallelism comes, therefore, as a surprise. But perhaps it should not. The Christian Eucharist seems to write large the most common and ordinary struggles of community-in-the-making. Though its leader differed (in this case the leader being Bob) and its task differed, the Eucharist group seemed to be in the other respects like the Eucharist, almost despite itself.

In any case, our reflection on the theology of the Eucharist can be extended. On the large scale, the leadership of Jesus, his work in the Last Supper and his presence in word and symbol in our liturgy today, is the key to our community. Jesus explains the Father and his own identity in relation to the Father. He experiences the cost of creative choice and interdependence. His becoming himself is a gift to us, the world-group who witness his dramatic passage to the Father, the source of all creativity. Our communion with him can be the source of our becoming ourselves and of bringing unity to all.

VI

The
ordination
group

TI. BACKGROUND*

en people are in a room. Nine of them, for whatever reason, feel in conscience that they have a standing duty occasionally to focus their attention toward the tenth. Let us call this tenth person the official of the group. The ten may be of varied personality and talent. They may be equally articulate and responsible. There may be grades of spiritual dedication and insight among them. Their personal histories may vary from rich to bleak. Their family backgrounds will range from the disrupted to the contented. All will have struggled with issues of self-esteem, personal worth and social confidence. There will be likes and dislikes. Each will understandably have life and contacts "outside" the room.

Let us suppose that the ten have something to do in common. This might be an external production, or it might be something to be done with respect to each other. In either case, the position of the official vis-à-vis the other nine suddenly comes under scrutiny. For his position seems advantageous in whatever proceedings take place. When the official speaks, he has, as it were, *guaranteed* attention. When one of the nine speaks, no such guarantee exists, and therefore attention paid him seems at best *haphazard*. The first thing to note, then, is that the official seems to have a *positional advantage*. Not that what he says will be truer, wiser, kinder, more closely attached to the common purpose of the moment, or anything else. But because of his advantageous positioning, it will *seem to claim such qualities*. His opinion will seem to encroach upon the opinions of others, his competence will seem larger, even though, on the merits of what actually gets said or contributed, nothing of the sort is the case.

*See p. 10.

What, then, is he doing "there"? How did he get "there"? Is his presence "there" harmful or helpful to the common pupose of the moment? These are the kinds of questions that arise when the nine taste the negative experience of their own lack of guaranteed position. Where did they pick up their "standing duty occasionally to focus their attention toward the tenth member"?[1] Was it through some charismatic appeal of the official? Some special competence? Was it because someone outside the room told them to do so? Was it through some original inattention or misunderstanding? Come to think of it, what possible value could there be in having such a person in the room?

Or does the official have some power of decision over the other nine, in their intramural dealings and in their outside ventures? What is the extent and scope of these powers, and what is their utility? Will his decisions be too frequent, too subjectively motivated, too confining or taxing? And in what sense do they "bind" the group? His presence seems to pose a constant challenge to the others, either to stay or to leave the group. That is, does "binding" have to do finally with maintaining the very existence of the group? And does this leave the nine with anything more than the individual decision to come or go, with no other scope or creativity to their individual decision?

Faced with these questions, the options are predictable. The nine can break up or leave. They can mope, and exaggerate the sense of their own impotence. They can claim the privileged position for themselves. They can attack it and render it useless (in which case, since they do not yet know *what* its use *is,* this can only look like an attack on the official's person). They can so exalt his position by attributing to it every sort of responsibility and talent imaginable that it becomes unbearable for him. Or they can clarify the competence of the official vis-à-vis their own.

* * * * *

What we have been trying to describe is the position of any official in any community. For the theology of priesthood has at the heart of it the simple fact that priests (pope, bishops) are and function as officials in the Christian community. All the pious accretions, all the shamanism, the undue reverence and the egalitarian humility, are not only distractions from that simple fact, they are also subversions of it. The nature of officialness, its uses and function, is what any theology of the priesthood must come to grips with.

To put the matter bluntly, if we leave God out of it for the moment, there is no difference between what happens when a priest baptizes and what happens when a non-priest does, save in the officialness of the former action. There is no difference between a priest forgiving and a non-priest forgiving, save in the officialness of the former forgiving. The witness of the priest at a sacramental marriage differs in no way from the witness of the others present except in the officialness of his act of witnessing. The priest's consolation of the sick and dying is exactly the same as anyone else's, except in its official quality. The priest officially recalls the Last Supper of Jesus, while the others present do so unofficially; nothing more is implied as far as recalling goes.[2] The official communication of the Holy Spirit (formerly through the Bishop alone but now also through the priest) differs not at all from the normal activity of communicating the Spirit to each other which ordinary Christians do unofficially. It matters little whether the community ordains someone or whether a Bishop does, save in the officialness of the product. The preaching of a priest is only an official version of the preaching of the ordinary Christian. Popes solemnly define things officially, whereas most of us never achieve official status for our solemn definitions. What marks the priest, then, and clearly constitutes the issue of his priesthood, is his official character. In the simplest terms and on first blush, it looks as though the sacrament of orders is the point where this official character is conferred on an individual.

Nor does it help to say that it is *God's* action in and through the priest that is the critical factor in his functioning. The fact that God is involved is not unique to priesthood. Even the fact that God's special promise attaches to the activity of priests is not all that decisive for our understanding. The question is rather: to *what* is God attaching his special promise? And if God seems to be attaching his sacramental promise to the existence and activity of an *official* in the community, then *we must ask what God sees in such official doings.* Or are we to suppose that his promise attaches to the priest in some purely arbitrary and otherwise senseless manner? We have to ask why it is a godly thing to ordain officials in the sacrament of orders, and to have these officials function so pervasively in all the other sacraments.

All this seems to run counter to our normal fantasies about priesthood, or at least to the high expectations that some have of priests. Some of us have thought that priests were different in a spiritual sense, and it seems that now we are describing them in a way that does away with an "essential" quality of their priesthood. Even these misgivings are revealing. We act as though officialness were not enough, not exciting, not productive dramatically or among the kind of things that would interest a person like Jesus. And it is so easy to caricature this emphasis on officialness. We immediately conjure up images of bureaucrats, establishment types, company men, officious people with safe positions, grinding systems of administrative decision, of descending rules and ascending appeals, talented people whose unique abilities are exploited and compromised, untalented people whose mediocrity is sanctioned and loosed upon others. We can stay with these fantasies and stereotypes, or we can push ahead and try to capture the positive humanistic value that resides in officialness.[3]

What difference, then, does officialness make? First of all, officials would be neither desirable nor necessary except for *community* purposes, for the pursuit of communal goals. So if the sacrament of orders is attributed to Jesus' institution, we are thereby making a statement about Jesus' attitude toward community. We already touched on this subject in our consideration of baptism. There are, however, two ways in which Jesus' emphasis on community can be conceived. It can be traced to a divine and sovereign overview by him of our creaturely needs. Or it can be traced to his human personality, and understood by analogy with other instances of community-mindedness that we have in life.

There are some people we know who simply think big, on a scale that frightens the average person. They spontaneously think not in terms of isolated, individual events that they wish to foster, remedy, or influence; they think in terms of national or international influence, of total markets, vast systems, of all future and possible instances of the thing that interests them. Great industrialists, statesmen, international competitors, educational innovators—many such people share this sense of scale in their outlook. Think of Francis Xavier, who felt he must "do China" before he could "get at" Japan in his missionary effort. The thought is numbing. This kind of vast vision has a human quality, whatever its spiritual motivation; it is often the fruit of temperament and inclination. And where it occurs it usually includes an organizational mentality, a determination to sustain the vision with practical, orderly steps. To do otherwise would be naive and even ludicrous.

There is a kind of reluctance to attribute to Jesus' humanity this kind of vision and this kind of hard-headed practicality. The vision was there, the movement, the impatience. A good part of his dealings with his followers, as we saw in our consideration of confirmation, took the form of organizing and outfitting them. At a certain point, personalities do not count for him. They must yield to the demands of the community's growth and development.

The priest is called upon to share in this community-wide vision of Jesus. This means *his concentration* will be on the *community dimension* of Christian living. He will have to see individual events in the light of total possibilities; to think of the intricate channels and criss-crossings whereby contact occurs or is blocked between different parts of the community; to be on the lookout for repercussions, good and bad; to observe the presence of inequality and diversity, of isolation and private interest; to feel along with the mass as it struggles for unity; to learn the conditions of consensus: compromise, diplomacy, arm-twisting, enticements, threats, and sweet reason. Above all, he has to distinguish in his head between his personal preference and what community-wide cohesion and welfare require.

But do not others in the community besides priests do these kinds of things? And often do them better? Why is the priest so special in doing them? In part, the answer is simply because that is his job. Interest, inclination, concern, charism, or spontaneity, while they may make him better at the job, do not serve to describe the job itself of *sustaining the community-wide vision.* No more than those qualities would define the job of a plumber or a policeman. More importantly, others in the community recognize that as the job. They know, or are reminded, that *the community dimension* which surrounds and pervades all their individual activities *is stated in the official on a standing basis* and as a *specific concentration.*

Whatever community concern or perceptivity or judgment others in the community might have is simply not *"read"* by the community in the same way. The official is *expected* to "say" the *community in all its dimensions* by virtue of his office. He is therefore *authorized,* however inarticulately, by the community in *this* competence, with no disrespect to the competence of others in countless other areas. If the community does not so authorize the priest, his job is rendered impossible or at least more difficult. If the priest neglects this role vis-à-vis the community to try his hand at other roles, sooner or later he will be driven back to it if he is to discover his uniqueness and identity as a priest.

It is easy to be distracted from this understanding of the matter. For, in these issues the argument is not so much about *what* priesthood is but about *how one becomes* an official in this community.[4] We will not make women officials. In much of the Church we will not make anyone an official who does not accept the law of celibacy. Religious in the Church cannot figure out whether they want to be all that official, whether their semi-official status compromises much of what they want to do. Some official statuses are being dropped (minor orders, subdiaconate) while others are growing (diaconate). Where the means and methods of becoming official are already (and understandably) in the hands of officials, there is understandable nervousness all around.

Few people have the patience to reflect on the difference between being an official and becoming one, between the job and how one gets the job. Many want official status by a private fiat. Then they are disappointed when the community does not recognize their claim to officialness. Yet, as we have seen, this recognition is essential to the workings of officialness. Others acquire a certain official standing in a subgroup of the wider community, among those similarly inclined or of the same persuasion. But this ends in cliques, sects, and faddish partisan movements.

Where the crisis of priesthood continues, it is usually in circumstances where the crisis of community is still stirring, if it has not run down from sheer exhaustion. The major disadvantage of priests is that from their vantage point they get a good official view of the lack of community, the community of which they are supposed to be the focuses. They are forced to ask themselves, What am I doing in a position which is built on the presupposition of community as a foundation, if that very community is rife with dissention, fragmentation, apathy, painful variation, separatist privilege, and so forth? Is not the "statement" of officials concerning the community-dimension a falsification of reality? If priests are supposed to "say" community, how is it that community does not yet exist?

The priest's spiritual faith is molded by how he looks on community. If he doubts the desirability or possibility of that community, then his position inevitably will become one of prestige, power and control. Or he will put impossible demands of quality leadership upon himself, thinking that he has to be a better Christian, a better practitioner of the virtues or of the sacramental arts than the layman. Instead of vigorously resisting this kind of paternalism, he will too often take upon himself the irresponsibilities of the community. At that point he becomes the most likely of scapegoats, expressing in himself the failures of others or their nervousness or pessimism concerning community. In the end, the priest's prayer of faith has to be no different than the original one: that they may be one.

Meanwhile, the priesthood goes on. Its existence is both crucial and, from a different perspective, not all that important. It is crucial in that it is a key means of reminding us all that the community-dimension is part of Jesus' vision of things. It tells us that the isolated case of goodness, justice, and virtue, while excellent in itself, is not the same as striving after these things on scale. The presence of officials in a community does not guarantee success in achieving results on a grand scale. But *it does guarantee a reminder that scale is desirable.* For, the very presence of the official, on whom individuals have "a standing duty occasionally to focus their attention," sets those individuals in motion as to *their* relation to the community-dimension of things. In the community-person, which the priest by definition is, Christians see their individual religious striving as *member*ship in community, with its vigorous demand for interrelating, for mutuality, for common identity, for coming to terms with differences of culture, pace, temperament, charism, and doctrine.

The unimportance of officialness lies in the fact that it is not the end of the world if, in all our activities, we do not achieve a community dimension. Where the goal of community itself is the greater enrichment of more individuals, then individual enrichment is clearly the greater good. So that, where it occurs, there can only be cause for rejoicing.

What we are implying throughout is that all the sacraments are community-dimension realities. There is an attempt going on *there,* in sacraments, to be concerned with scale, with a vision of broad possibilities, with a common and multiple urging. To *such* strivings the Christian attests that God's favor is especially—sacramentally— promised. Not that that favor cannot be operative in other situations; not even that the community perspective is nobler or higher or absolutely essential. But it is the community perspective that the priest announces by his presence in sacramental situations. And it is that perspective that the community supports when, through ordination, the community receives a new official in its midst.

II. THE GROUP EVENT

Our overall task is to study how our being in a group
influences what eventually gets said about God,
Jesus, sacraments, or, especially in this case,
the sacrament of orders.
To this end the group is to ordain
one of its members, with the proviso that it first
shares the responsibility of explaining
to the candidate what is thereby involved.

The ordination group manifested six major concerns. First, from the very beginning the group expressed misgivings about being **competent to ordain** anyone. These misgivings stemmed, it was maintained, from the fact that the community had for so long a time been denied any voice in the selection of priests. How, then, could they now be asked to ordain someone? How would they know the criteria? *Anger was being vented here, partly at their inexperience, but partly at the facilitator who set them this task.* Stu, in particular, felt that any choosing done by the group would be ineffectual, since it would be deprived of official status, would not have the "chains" of tradition behind it, and would most likely be taken as heresy.

"Official status" seemed, at this point, terribly inflated. Some potent and magical quality was being attributed to it, in comparison to which the group's own efforts seemed pitifully small. *Stu's stance probably referred as much to the group-life as to the theological issue of priesthood. He was, in a way, asking whether the facilitator would recognize what the group came up with, and whether the members themselves would recognize and accept each other as they worked on the task. But by inflating the notion of "official" at this early stage, he was certainly making it hard for the group whose task it was to select one of its own members for that very inflated job. In any case, this denial of its own competence by the group caused much scuttling of the task in the early stage of the session.*

Second, the group felt duty bound to make the priest someone who would **meet the needs of the community.** The candidate would have to be someone who responded to those needs, measuring his own authorization for his job by what the needs of the community dictated. Especially important was the need of the community to be free, that is, not to have to avail themselves of his services or his position. Any coercion on his part was to be rejected. Joe staunchly projected this interpretation of priesthood: the priest was to "educe" the community, taking people from where they were "toward the oncoming Christ."

Third, and in contrast to the foregoing concern, was the group's desire to **adapt itself** to the desires and talents of whichever **individual** might be the candidate. It was as though the candidate would define the parameters of priesthood by his own interest, ability, holiness, and choice. A person should be sought for the job who "seems good at it." He should be given considerable latitude in determining his mode of operation especially in the matter of celibacy.

Under this rubric of "the candidate's desires," some issues of the group-life were also being worked out: (1) the members of the group were sizing each other up, probing each other's inclinations; (2) the group was warning against repression of any kind toward its members; (3) a vehicle was being provided for individuals in the group to express those endowments which they would require from any potential candidate.

Fourth, and somewhere between the last two concerns, the group was anxious about the **permanency** of the priest's commitment to the community. The complaint was that priests move from community to community at too great a pace, thus neglecting the community's needs. But the underlying concern seemed to be more generalized. There seemed to be implied a demand on the priest to be dramatically effective in the lives of others; by virtue of his own personal dedication and desire, he is expected to be a stable influence on the community.

Fifth, the group seemed reluctant to say that the priest **was in any way "different."** This was the clearest and most constant problem that agitated the group, the fear of making the priest out to be better than anyone else or of allowing him to be special. The first half of the session was especially marked with this issue. Three lay members of the group (Stu, Grace, and Joe) did most of the talking during this period. *The group provided them with a foil* in Sarah, who defended the most "clerical" view of priest: the priest is called to extraordinary services; he had to have been a decent boy (*sic*); he was all things to all men, and so forth. Sarah herself had always wanted to be a priest ("until," as she would later say, "this session"). In contrast, Stu preferred to talk of the community itself as priest. Grace assigned the priest a few "churchy" things to do, but for the rest she would want him to be like anyone else. She stressed that the priest was not the only leader in the parish. Joe had the most roundabout way of voicing his fears of clerical difference. He himself was soon to become a permanent deacon. He felt that one in such a position was more to be confided in by people than the priest, "because you're a lay person . . . and you're married." Joe thought people would get a greater sense of community solidarity from a permanent deacon. He viewed the priest as a facilitator in the parish, and not the only one at that. He opposed all hierarchial thinking as a violation of a sense of community.

There were holes in this thinking that the group were not facing. Joe himself had admitted, "yet once a permanent deacon is ordained he is no longer a lay person." He also freely stated that the permanency of the diaconate does not foreclose "cutting out with one's family to another parish." He even volunteered that talk of team ministry (where there was no hierarchy) was vague. The most the facilitator could do at this point was to ask the group whether it was airing "gripes" or ventilating anger through these comments. The response to this was twofold: *there was a sudden confusion in the group as to what its task was; the group began to imagine that it was supposed to be "ordaining someone, but not specifically as priest."* Secondly, *Joe, Stu, and Grace began to attack Sarah* for what they considered her high expectations of priests. They made the point vigorously that many former sinners had turned out to be excellent priests. Nothing was said about unrepentant sinners who were still priests.

The exchange between the advocates of the laity and Sarah was unproductive. Only Betty was trying to work constructively during it. The facilitator finally asked if all in the group were working on the task, whereupon Joan, Gerry, Alice, and Lena began to speak up.

Their contributions led the group to a different concern which we will consider subsequently. But it was noteworthy that, *after this point, the group talked about the "specialness" of the priest more gingerly.* It was careful to stress that the priest was not better than anyone else, nor above, nor apart. Lena lapsed occasionally into making high "claims for/demands upon" the priest, but in general the group was more businesslike in trying to work out how the priest differed from the rest of the community in what he did. Stu admitted frankly that it was easy to be jealous of the priest's "status."

Several descriptions of priesthood were rejected as not being peculiar to priests: that the priest was "aware of the community's ideals," that he would "point out areas where love was lacking" in the community, that he was "the great lover" in the community. Several suggestions about the priest were left hanging: that he was an "official," that he was a "public" person, that he did his job on a "full-time" basis, that he was to "raise consciousness" in the community. Betty wisely remarked that the group was worried about the accountability of the priest. If the group had a priest in its midst they would want to know how to judge his or her accountability, and hence would not feel so victimized by the priest's "apartness."

Sixth, *the reason why the group could move out of its earlier dilemma (either the community decides what the priest is, or the priest himself decides) was because the group finally got around to seeking some input for its task from the tradition.* We have mentioned how this began after Joan and the others entered the discussion at the point where it was deadlocked around the issue of the specific difference of the priest. *The appeal to tradition helped dispel some of the fantasy and bad feelings about the specialness of the priest.* Who, after all, could argue with the fact that Jesus might have had something in mind by instituting a priesthood? **What** Jesus might have had in mind was another question. The group spoke of Jesus' institution of priesthood as "not leaving things to chance," as "making sure," as giving "strength" to the community to do the same things he did, even as giving the community "the right" to do what he did. None of these comments tell us very much about what Jesus understood by priests. They seem in fact to imply that the community cannot be trusted. The group found it difficult to locate its own responsibility and authority whenever Jesus' view of priests was being discussed. Sarah caught this feeling in her remark, "Jesus knows our needs better than we do." But just how the priesthood was connected with Jesus' wise foresight never did emerge from the group.

III. THEOLOGICAL IMPLICATIONS

First, we might examine some implications of the way the group spoke about the "call" to priesthood. The expression was not a casual or neutral one in the group. Rather, it functioned differently according to the group's handling of different issues. When the group was resenting its own responsibility for, and involvement in, the process of choosing priests, God's "call" was invoked in this sense: the *community* cannot have a voice because *God* is calling. Or, if the candidate seemed to be deciding too much for himself what priesthood was about, the group referred to God's "calling" in another sense: individuals should listen to God's call, and not think (as though God never called us to think). Again, "call" was used in a more straightforward way to describe the community's action of presenting its candidate for ordination to the bishop. In the end the group settled for a kind of dual calling, God's and the community's. What was striking in all of this was the futility of the expression "call," when no description was being offered of *what* someone was called to do or to be. The picture of God calling someone in a kind of vague or general way is frightening, if not subtly violent. And yet, that is how vocation language can sound if nothing more is added.

Behind the confusion about "calls" is the question of how someone gets to be authorized in this community to be its official. We will consider later in this book problems which surround the issue of authorization, and how someone has to have a clear idea of what role he has in the community, whether the community accepts him in that role, and so forth. The peculiar problem of "calls" to the priestly vocation is that, through them, one is being authorized in a role which encompasses and affects all others in the community. Hence, there is a lot at stake, and people naturally want to know who is calling whom and how someone gets such a widely ranging role without some equally wide process of consultation. That Jesus might have wanted such persons in the community is soon forgotten. So is the presumed agreement by all in the community that what Jesus wants they are to want also. At any rate, some of the ambiguity about divine calls stems from this question of authorization and acceptance by the community.

Apart from the matter of God's calling, language about God was conspicuous in the ordination group by its absence. Is that what happens when we suddenly realize that God's calling is more often than not a calling *together?*

Celibacy also figured as an issue in the group. In fact, the session ended with a serious headcount in process about where the group stood on the celibacy issue. Throughout the session, the celibacy discussion seemed to function in two ways: in the first, the issue was whether we should respect an individual's inclinations in the matter of the *style* of living the priesthood. But in the second, the issue carried further. At stake was whether individual judgments about the *nature* of priesthood itself were legitimate. The group seemed eager to define priesthood with no reference to celibacy. This very haste, however, makes one pause. A question seemed called for: can one do *this kind of thing* if one is married? Can one authentically and undividedly be a community-dimension person where a spouse is involved? Can one "say" the whole community without blurring, and without distraction for others in the community, other than by being alone?

There is no doubt that frequently it is the irrational demands of the community that call for a celibate clergy (when the community requires total commitment to itself, unreal virtue in its officials, magical efficacy and ritual purity for all its operations). We also know of many married officials, religious and secular, whose authority seems in no way compromised by their married status. Still, in the light of the group experience, we are led to ask whether the connection between celibacy (not the law, but the reality) and priestly ministry is more intrinsic and meaningful than is generally allowed.

Lastly, the group seemed to settle most easily into a view of priesthood which underscores the eucharistic function of priests. This phenomenon might simply reflect the fact that people come into contact with priests most frequently and most visibly in that setting. But it might also mean that the role and function of the priest as a community-dimension person is *verified* most manifestly when the community, whose focus the priest is, *gathers itself* to Christ and *says itself* through the crucial yet modest mechanism of a priest.

VII

The
marriage
group

W I. BACKGROUND*

hen a Christian goes to a wedding, he should enjoy himself and keep the wine flowing. The tradition is clear on that much. But when a wedding goes Christian, the couple should expect to receive a lot of gratuitous input from the Christians present concerning what is or is supposed to be transpiring. For, by the sacrament of marriage, love becomes an issue. Where something is an issue, debate is predictable and discernment necessary. The Christian community does not see marriage as something to be taken for granted. Where Christian marriage is concerned, the spontaneity, sincerity and inclinations of the marrying couple suddenly become buffeted by forces far more complex than would be anticipated.

Some (just some) *of the questions* that surround the issue of the sacrament of marriage are the following:

Who should marry?
Who should marry whom?
Who decides who should marry?

*See p. 10.

What are the actual reasons people marry?
Are there economic pressures on people to marry?
Do these pressures affect men and women equally?
Are there social pressures on people to marry?
To what extent is marriage an escape from the parental home?
To what extent is marriage playing at being grown up?
To what extent is marriage testing out one's fledgling wings?

Is loneliness a sufficient reason to marry?
Is marriage necessary for career advancement?
Are people made for each other?
Is romance necessary for marriage?
Should marriage partners be friends?
Can wives have good men friends?
Can husbands have good women friends?
Does marriage narrow the range of friendships?
Does Christian marriage narrow the range of friendships?
Is a life-long commitment possible?

Is a life-long commitment desirable?
Is a life-long commitment fun?
What is the connection between love and marriage?
What if one has gotten married for the wrong reasons?
Who is to judge what the right reasons for marrying are?
Is marriage the only means of self-fulfillment?
How are those who do not marry treated in our culture?
Is one age better than another for getting married?
Do most married people really marry?
Does marriage include parenthood?

Do parents also need to be married?
What preparation should be made for bringing children into the
    world?
What preparation is usually made?
What does the upbringing of children consist of?
Are there wrong reasons for having children?
Do parents have any responsibility for children's relation to God?
Is love possible where children are ruled out?
What does birth control do to marriage?
What birth regulation is required by marriage?
Do parents act out their own problems through their children?

What is being aborted in an abortion?
Are there parallels to abortion in general human relations?

What are people's rights in the matter of sexual relations?
Can one discuss abortion apart from the previous question?
Why do Church people discuss them separately?
How do moral rights differ from legal rights?
What percentage of people understand the difference?
Do people insist on responsibilities as much as on rights?
How are love and permanent commitment related to sex?
What sex is God?

How does pre-marital sex differ from marital sex?
Is pre-marital sex a failure of nerve?
Is marriage a failure of nerve?
Do people express their fear of death through sex?
Does Christianity make sex better?
What of homosexual marriages?
What are impediments to marriage?
What are the impediments to a sacramental marriage?
Who caused these impediments originally?
What kind of God is envisioned in the sacrament of marriage?

Who knows more about love, man or God?
Is love a spontaneous instinct or something that must be learned?
Who can answer these questions?
Should the Church have anything to say about marriage?
Did Jesus institute the sacrament of marriage?
How could Jesus know anything about love?
What do other religions say about marriage?
What do other cultures say about marriage?
What are the ethnic influences on marriage?
Is a marriage automatically Christian because it is ethnic?

Do people usually mean the sacrament of marriage when they say
    marriage?
What about the role of personal conscience in marriage?
What about the role of Jesus in personal conscience?
What does the Old Testament teach about marriage?
Does Christian marriage demand a certain educational level?
Does Christian marriage demand a certain cultural milieu?
Should couples be charged money for receiving the sacrament?
Will people marry in heaven?
Are marriage and the religious life incompatible in the same person?
What are the advantages of Christian marriage?

What are the disadvantages of Christian marriage?
Is marriage beneficial to society?
Is marriage beneficial to the Christian community?
Is the family the basic unit of the Christian community?
Is it normal that families break up over Jesus?
Does celibacy tell married people anything?
Does celibacy make Jesus distrusted?
Can one partner so outgrow the other that they are no longer
   married?
What percentage of sacramental marriages are easy to annul?
Do people understand the difference between divorce and
   annulment?

Is the consummation of a marriage part of the sacrament?
Is monogamy a law of nature or of Jesus?
Can a polygamous person really love?
Are marriage vows more binding than religious vows?
Why do marriages fail?
Can anyone judge whether a sacramental marriage has taken place?
Is it a contradiction to say a Catholic's second marriage is
   sacramental?
Can people live with contradictions?
Can second marriages be good without being sacramental?
Do people care what Jesus might have had in mind about marriage?
Can the sacrament of marriage be explained to people about to
   marry?

We do not think, nor would anyone reasonably demand, that
couples put all these questions to themselves at the point of receiving
the sacrament of marriage. We are not saying that couples should
face the issue of marriage in all its detail. We are saying that the
issue of marriage faces the couple, whether the couple is aware of it
or not.

But people do not cope with such complicated issues as the present one simply by thinking about them. Their very complexity warns
us against that. Issues are resolved rather *by the company we keep*
than by our prowess at logical assessment. What the sacrament of
marriage provides a couple is the right company in which to work
out problems connected with the issue of marriage. Let us admit
immediately that people generally want more than companionship in
the search of the truth. They want the right answers. They want to be
absolutely sure of the correctness of what they are doing. They approach the sacrament of marriage with this mindset, expecting it to
satisfy the necessity of being correct, from every aspect. But they do

not wish to be otherwise exposed to the conflicting input, challenging views, uneven support, inconclusive example, frayed faith, and
enigmatic developments which all come from the *persons* whose
company the sacrament of marriage provides them with. So our talking about the sacrament becomes somewhat defensive: We must indicate the advantages and value of discovering love in the company
envisioned in the sacrament of marriage.

A. Central to that company is the person of Jesus. Jesus is sought out
as the expert on love, who most knows the ways of his Father's kind
of love. Whether or not the couple who marries thinks that love must
be learned is a critical matter for the sacrament of matrimony. If it
need not be learned, if there is no theoretical possibility of expertise
in love, then there is truely no place for the sacrament of marriage.
Jesus would be left no other role in Christian marriage than that of a
friendly booster. But where we depend on Jesus both to discover
what love is and to have God's powerful promise of assistance in
achieving love, then the sacrament's role is meaningful. It is a protestation of our dependence, not in any way that shames us or makes
us obsequious, but with dignified recognition of the realities involved.
    But what are Jesus' qualifications? What is his familiarity with
love? Can he, if he was not married, serve as a model for love
between husband and wife? We tend to think of the latter kind of
love as so specific, so tied to our bodiliness, to our life in a family, to
our agonies and joys with this person, that Jesus' kind of love is eyed
suspiciously as not dealing with the same problem. Marriage is a
matter of singling out. There is the astonishing centering of one
person on one other, electing, settling upon this one, ruling out
others, seemingly ignoring them, the fascination and narrowing of
focus, the outpouring of dedication in one direction, the concentration and intimate pact. How can Jesus address himself to this centered love when his kind of love looks so diffuse, so expansive and
all-embracing, so wide-ranging and quick to move further? Is it that
we are merely saying that Jesus has some knowledge of the *common*
aspects of love, those which apply in every instance of love and
therefore also in the case of married love? Even in saying this, we
would be putting Jesus at some distance from married love, since
"common aspects" can so easily be taken to mean aspects which do
not really matter or do not help all that much in the *specific* matter of
married love. We are tempted to cut back his contribution to the
Christian's married love, to attribute to him only a needed divine
empowerment but nothing in the way of a commentary on married
love, no insight into it, nor real appreciation of the kind of love that
married people need.

The previous remarks leave us with a sense of diffidence about Jesus' role in matrimony. We can get mired down in that diffidence, or we can examine in closer detail *what there is about Jesus' love that speaks to the issue of marriage*.

1. There is the style of his initial involvement with people. He does not expect that all can be said at once. He gives relationships time. Accompaniment is the condition of developing close ties. Yet, he is not shy. He offers contact with himself. He promises excitement and worth in his company. Initially, he makes the other person's future important, that something will become of them.

2. As the relationship develops, communication is important. He tells his friends what is most important to him. All that he knows he shares. He is open about his feelings and exposes himself to others in that respect. He feels the feelings of others. He goes aside with his friends, and he goes aside away from his friends. He prays with them, revealing that most private side of himself to them. He takes his friends' part in controversy, using his talents to turn aside criticism of them. Yet, he argues with them, insults them, gets furious and sarcastic with them. He tries to keep them real, attacking their false hopes and naiveté. He is sensitive to their family ties without rearranging the world in the name of those ties. His communication is not heavily direct. He uses that most polite way of talking about others, through stories and imaginative illustrations which keep a merciful distance while drawing close to the point. At other times, he can dwell bluntly on people's shortcomings. He encourages others and begs for their help, but he does not make his success as a person depend finally on them.

3. He keeps identities intact. He is who he is and others are who they are. The union of his love and friendship with them does not blur, in fact it increases, the diversification of identities. A fisherman becomes *the* fisherman. A carpenter becomes *the* carpenter. A doubter becomes *the* doubter. A traitor becomes *the* traitor. A prostitute becomes *the* prostitute. A rich man becomes *the* rich man. A mother becomes *the* mother. This sharpening of personalities is not simply the byproduct of his notoriety. Rather, the reverse is true. His notoriety is the fruit of his ability to call others to be most themselves. He knows who he is. People can make him rabbi, but not king. They can make him master, but only so far. They can call him good, but not in order to play games. Who he is is jealously defended by him; it preoccupies him. But this does not blur who others are. The hero-worshipers themselves become heroes, subtly and without

their noticing it. He talks of vast harvests, of the fate of whole nations, of general outcomes, of choices made on a cosmic scale, but the end result is paradoxically the greater individualization of his followers.

4. The basis of his relationship with others involves more than his *person* alone or theirs alone. There is a work to be done in common. Social responsibility, mission, and concern for others flow from any relationship he has with someone. Mutual contemplation is not an end in itself for him. Love takes shape within activities, plans, controversies, and movements.

5. His special loves fit together with his more general ones, if not harmoniously, then, at least with determination on his part and with a lack of apology. His relationship to his Father is all-consuming. That is his great and most chosen love. He loves his mother and brethren, despite the jarring complications that arise where relatives are concerned. He loves some disciples more than others. He has to maneuver among the reactions of people to his seeming preferences. He shows that singling out can be an authentic quality of all love, that it does not entail a lack of fidelity to people but is rather the source of a greater fidelity.

6. He experiences the rougher aspects of love. He knows the suffering of not being loved in return. He identifies himself with others' sinfulness and failure. He risks betrayal. He tries to forgive the unforgiving. He has to stare at the backs turned on him, to talk to feigned incomprehension. He knows what leave-taking is and what returning can mean. He senses the sneers at the company he keeps. He is used by others and is probably tempted to use them (for an example, an illustration, a sermon theme, a target against which to rally his own) rather than to love them. He can put the best face on the worst doings. He can preach love when little evidence for it is forthcoming.

All these qualities of Jesus' kind of love seem to have their obvious parallel in married love. We feel that the distinction made earlier between the so-called common aspects of love and the specific aspects of married love is flimsier than it at first appears and that there are few problems connected with the common aspects of love that do not reappear in the case of married love.

B. Jesus is not the only company envisioned in the sacrament of marriage. There is the Christian community. Jesus serves as its model, to be sure. Married love in that community patterns itself, in the sense developed above, after his kind of love. But the discovery, analysis, and articulation of "his kind of love" in relation to marriage is itself a complicated business, left in large part in the questionably competent hands of those who are trying to love him. Even the privileged record of his love that we find in Scripture is tied to the times of those who composed the Scripture. Problems connected with marriage which did not exist then and have since emerged demand a continuous reflection on the part of the Christian community. The first role of the community, then, is to help *interpret* in an ongoing fashion how Jesus' kind of love can be a model for married love.

This interpretation is not an untroubled process. In the long tradition of interpretation, various issues arise, some abruptly and shiningly new, others predictable to the point of being tiresome, still others with chronic irregularity. The reaction is accordingly tortuous. It is often defensive and plainly partisan. It is frequently heroic. It must be discerning and decisive and hence is prone to be sharp. It is often flawed.

Over the years there has been an *official* interpretation which can be gathered from church documents, solemn and otherwise, and which provides a picture of how the officials think marriage is to look when modeled after Jesus. Emphasis in this interpretation lies on the indissolubility of marriage, on the rejection of contraceptive intent and practice, on the rights of parents as the educators of their children, on the absolute immorality of abortion, on the value of mutual example in marriage, and so forth. This official interpretation stresses the exemplarity of the Holy Family, and its premise seems to be that the family is the basic unit of Christianity, envisioned by Jesus as *the* building block of a growing kingdom. While this impression does not leap out of the New Testament, it makes a certain amount of sense from a practical standpoint.

Unofficial interpretations by the Christian community of how Jesus' kind of love relates to marriage range from the theologically learned to the popular. Here the emphasis lies on the relationship between the spouses, on premarital problems, on living out a Christian marriage in a culture which often does not reinforce it, on financing family life, on the needs of children for their proper development, and so forth. A celibate officialdom is less likely to focus on these problems. On the other hand, this unofficial interpretation has its version of the exemplarity of the Holy Family mentioned above. For, marriage seems to be discussed and assessed mainly through the eyes of the children: potential influences on the children, the effect of culture on the children, the religious training of children, even the regulation of interparental relationships for the good of the children.

At times it seems that the adult population has given up on itself, so interested is it in talking about marriage solely in terms of the children's problems. While such concern most assuredly could be the expression of authentically overflowing marital love, it sometimes seems to be a circuitous way for parents to deal with the difficulties of working out their adult relationships with each other and with the world.

Unofficial and official interpretations of Christian marriage certainly overlap. It would be simplistic to say that ordinary Christians have no other problem with divorce, abortion and birth control than the fact that the official Church harps on them. Even more simplistic is the attempt to drive a wedge between Jesus' kind of love and the interpretations of it, official or unofficial, which we are exposed to in the Church. The desire to be in immediate touch with Jesus' kind of love, so that one would never have to listen to other opinions, is tempting. It would be nice to say that love need not be learned in community. It would be pleasant to ignore the painful question of whether the likelihood of discovering love, or of discovering Jesus' kind of love, is increased in some communities rather than in others. Problems of faith hover just beneath the surface of the issue of sacramental marriage, and our faith in the Christian community is most tested. Like all Christian belief, the belief that the community officially and unofficially has an interpretative role in a couple's marriage demands that the believer suffer the interference of others. It calls for trusting that in others we will find some of the wisdom of Jesus' vision of love.

With this trusting and suffering encountered in a demanding community comes an unexpected resurrection for marriage. The couple acquires, through the sacrament, not only challenging interpretations but also reinforcement and support. This statement does not always fit the image or fantasy we have of each other in the Christian community. Many feel that they will indeed be challenged, even criticized and judged, but not positively buoyed or uplifted in any noticeable way. Here again our faith in the community is put to the test. For the support (example, sympathy, wisdom, listening, encouragement) we hope to find in the community is elusive. To find it, to find the humanly perceptible contacts that living the sacrament of marriage demands, we must enter that community with risk and boldness. We enter thereby an area where frightening (for faith) questions arise: Who prays? Who knows Jesus? Who is reliable? Who cares? Who will disagree with me without judging me? Who is practical? Who is prudent? Who will maintain the strained balance between doctrinal and pastoral concerns? Who will have the wisdom to tell me when I am wrong? Who can integrate my needs with the legitimate needs of the community? These problems of faith and trust in the community are inextricably connected with the sacrament of marriage as a favor done us by Jesus.

C. None of what has been said thus far should detract from the truth that, in the sacrament of marriage, a couple is also finding each other's company in a new way. By placing their love for each other in the Lord and in the community, they discover each other in new ways. The possibility of learning each other's faith and spiritual depth is there. So is the possibility of learning each other's doubts and shallows. Their love for one another acquires a new and explicit task, namely, to help each other grow in the Lord and in his Church. This tremendous ideal of acting as each other's liberator and catalyst in spiritual things awaits every couple through the sacrament of marriage.

* * * * *

The sense of responsibility that emerges from these pages is admittedly almost overwhelming. There seem to be just too many people who are involved with a couple's plans and intentions in marriage. Would not the couple be confused and depressed by such a cloud of witnesses? A few clear, firm and mechanical rules might better suit the marrying couple. Tell them what the rules are and let them decide to abide by them; that would be sacramental marriage. No nonsense about ongoing interpretation, challenge, and potential support. Sink or swim by the rules, without interference from anyone else (forgetting the original interference from the rulemakers). It is clear that couples cannot live consistently or honorably with this alternative. The issue of marriage is too complicated, the process whereby the rules are formed too fluid, the rules themselves too subject to pastoral development, the social responsibility too obvious for the sacrament of marriage to be reduced to some private and protective haven for the timid.

The probable reason people rush to the rules is because they have sensed the complexity of sacramental marriage and have been frightened by it. As in the case of many other sacraments, they fail to see the sacrament of marriage as a *beginning*. Even for commitments we have to distinguish the beginning, the middle and the end. Commitments propose, protest, and prophesy about the end, but they do not bring it about. Faith is closer to surmise than to knowledge, and commitments involve our faith about the final outcome. The Christian trusts that God can handle the future. He believes that God, although as serious about the rules as the next person, is better than the next person at picking up the pieces in an individual couple's lives. With everyone shouting what God will or will not do, it is understandable that placing marriage in his hands is a nervous business. Why begin anything so freighted with the intangible promise of God? Fears about infidelity reach right into our relationship with God. This situation serves again to show how fundamental attitudes toward God press upon our understanding of the sacrament of marriage. It takes a simple and generous faith to include his presence in one's married love.

Are there people of such faith around? We suggest that there are. People are not fools by nature, still less by grace. They can see through alternatives, such as the following alternative to the hard vision of sacramental marriage we have presented:

> Our basic attitude toward marriage is that we would like to try it out. We have already done so on an experimental scale, so that actually there will not be much added by a formal ceremony. We are here at this sacramental ceremony mainly to please our families. We value the family life that we had, but we also see its obvious cultural limitations and transient shape. As for our commitment, we realize that each of us can change, that our tastes and interests can develop along different, even divergent, lines. This might end our association some day, although we are willing to exert ourselves in the meantime to make the most of it. We even think that we need God's help for this. We do not believe anything about a natural law in the matter of marriage, since God deals with people as persons. We are both baptized Catholics. We think that Christ had a role in the social reorganization of men toward a better life, and with this much we agree. We believe that, had he lived longer, he would have married. His cultural background would inevitably make him insensitive to the role of woman in marriage. We prefer a more contractual arrangement in which the woman's place is assured. Because of the population explosion, and because of our career interests, we do not think it advisable to have children. Should we by chance have any, we would offer them every opportunity to exercise free choice in the matter of their religious commitment, something we feel we lacked. We had to lie in the questionnaire the priest gave us about our attitude on abortion, which we consider a private affair. We do not want to make sex as central to marriage as the Catholic Church does. However, we do not want, as a fixed rule, to limit our sexual possibilities to each other, if something else helps our growth and openness. It will not be difficult to sustain these resolves, since there are enough people around who think as we do to make them feasible.

This alternative, we suggest, is transparent to many Christians. Its caution is depressing. Its protectedness is sad, especially in the young. Its prognosis is that it is just a matter of time. It will be trapped by the very isolation it carves out. Its fear of inconsistency is poignant, since greater inconsistency is in store for it. It pretends to be more pragmatic than God, or more sophisticated—a fatal error in either case. It is humorless and bereft of emotional vulnerability. Most people would prefer to look like fools or sinners rather than face such an antiseptic fate. The task, then, is to seek out the company of fools and sinners. We will probably find Jesus there before us.

II. THE GROUP EVENT

The marriage group was structured somewhat differently from the other groups described in this study. It had the same overall purpose as the other groups, namely, to study the influence of being-in-a-group on what gets said theologically. Its specific theological task was to explain to a couple what the annulment of a sacramental marriage entails. A couple was provided to whom this explanation was to be offered. They were instructed by the facilitator simply to sit in the group without interacting with the others. In other words, they were to do nothing else than literally receive the explanation from the others. The purpose in this experiment was to test the responsibility of the group, to see how it would react to the presence of two silent people in its midst as it worked on its task. The silent couple also provided a visible sign of marriage in the group, which differs from other sacraments in that it involves more than one recipient or minister.

The task consisted of explaining annulment to the couple rather than directly explaining the sacrament of marriage. The idea behind this formulation of the task was to bring the experiment more quickly to the negative aspects of married love (or, more properly, of marrying people), as well as to its positive explanation. The facilitator thought that the group would have trouble with these negative aspects, with the possibility that something be lacking in a marriage. So he tried to reduce the chance that the group take off in the direction of a euphoric paean to romantic love by introducing the question of annulment into the task. It is important to note that **neither** of these ideas—the silent couple or the emphasis on annulment—may have been a good one. They were part of the experimental process in which trial and error normally figure. Yet they seemed to create, as we will describe, an inordinate amount of consternation in the group.

The very first speaker, Beatrice, addressed a question to the silent couple, Joe and Irene. When no response was forthcoming, Beatrice remarked, ''they're really not here.'' ''Or,'' she suggested, ''maybe it's too painful to talk about.'' *Her fantasy about the couple was shared by others*. The group argued among itself as to whether it could legitimately assume that Joe and Irene ''had a dilemma.''

106

Initially this created an impression of concern and sympathy for Joe and Irene, but we will see just how deep such sentiments ran. What was even more interesting was how *the couple's silence affected the group's ability to do the task.* Anne was the most outspoken about the couple's silence. She candidly admitted that she could not explain things to people without a personal response from the people to whom the explanation was being offered. She demanded some "contact," if giving the explanation was to make any sense to her. Obviously such contact was ruled out by the arrangement of the couple's silence. *The group, however, did not respond to Anne. It did not make "contact" with her—the very condition that she had just described as being important to her.* Instead, they "explained to" her how her request was impossible under the conditions of the task, and then, through Vic, turned to a more "objective" handling of the task. The facilitator let this work go on for a while and finally made reference to the possibility that there was an "annulment" going on in the group itself. Mary took this to refer to the relation of the group to Joe and Irene, but *this response was a denial of the more pressing problem of Anne.* Beatrice admitted this, saying "Anne makes me uneasy."

Anne, then, had a chance to repeat her problem with the silent couple. Unless the couple had scope for a personal response, any explanation offered them would seem "hierarchical, impersonal, bureaucratic and legislative," just as the Church tends to be. Vic again opposed this view, arguing for an objective way of handling the task. *Beatrice tried to be conciliatory.* She indicated that an impasse seemed to have been reached between Vic and Mary (*she meant Anne, but rather than mention that potentially painful clash she named Anne's most recent supporter, Mary*). She thought, however, that the group could still work as a community, "even with its two solemns." *Anne was not moved.* "We can only respond," she said, "if everyone is willing to come out and meet other people in the room." *Clearly, the silent couple was now functioning as a symbol for* **everyone's** *reticence.*

Harry pointed out again that Anne's desire to interact with Joe and Irene was outside the obvious arrangement of the task. "So your subjective thing has been eliminated, annihilated," he concluded to Anne. *At this, Anne raised a threat which she was later to carry out.* She suggested that the group could adopt the same tactic of silence itself, or that it could find some way of "reaching" Irene and Joe, perhaps non-verbally. She offered the group this alternative: either to treat their present situation the way "the organization as Church with its rules" would, or to act as a community, which would include the two people who were silent. Cis supported Anne to a degree. She said that "the kind of thing we are doing here" is reflective of what too often goes on in the Church, where couples "are talked at and about but not to." Beatrice agreed that it was hard to talk to "two statues." Perhaps encouraged by all this, Anne announced to all, and to the silent couple in particular, "I am keeping silence with you until you choose to speak. The responsibility for all three of our silences is now shared." With this, Anne said no more in the group.

How do we explain this development? Was Anne's problem the candid personal statement that it seemed to be, namely, that **she** needed a responsive listener before she could explain things? *Was she indirectly criticizing the facilitator's arrangement of the group, and challenging, even seeking,* **his** *authority? Was she really complaining about* **others** *in the group whom she did not consider honest and open in the discussion? Was she fearful of where an open discussion might lead? Was, finally, her concern with the* **wider Church** *which is pictured in somewhat bleak terms by her?* [The point here is not to discover which of these interpretations is the correct one, but rather to show how Anne's stand affected the language of the group as it described annulment.]

For, all during the time that Anne's issue was building up, *the group was also slowly composing a description* of what annulment means. First, a picture of sacramental marriage was provided. Mary called it a commitment made to God. The extent of the commitment would depend on "how much of a position the people were in to make that kind of commitment." Harry added that sacramental marriage also entailed some type of public commitment within the Christian community. Beatrice rounded out the picture by saying that a commitment between the marrying couple was also involved. Mary then began to urge a position on annulment that was to be central to the group's considerations throughout the task. "A commitment made by two people with God is best resolved there." An annulment cannot be limited to "that which is authorized by canon law." Because growth in maturity is so complicated, and because all our decisions are defective, "no set of laws or rules can judge better than a couple" anything about the marriage commitment.

The group responded to Mary in a tentative and kind way. Beatrice explained how annulment did not have to do with getting out of a marriage, but rather was a statement to the effect that no marriage had ever existed. Harry pointed out that civil law also used annulment in that sense, in cases, for example, of "mental deficiency." He granted that people could abuse the law by using it to their own advantage. But law, he said, "is an arbitrary set-up, because of groups."

The issue quickly came down to attitudes about community itself, which seemed to be the basis for the group's statements about annulment. Mary thought that marriage had to do with God and "hopefully, but not necessarily, with community." She invited the group to discuss annulment as it sees it, apart, as it were, from what the Church might mean by annulment. The group declined. Beatrice drew a parallel with other sacraments, asking Mary whether they too were private things between people and God, with no involvement by the community. *No one worked with Beatrice's suggestion.* Instead, the group argued about an intervention of the facilitator who had asked whether God or the community grants the annulment. "Grant" seemed a poor word to Beatrice. Normally it means "to offer a gift," and this could not be the case in an annulment! Harry preferred to talk of annulment as "a declaration in resume form of one's findings." Yet, this argument was only a *temporary distraction from the main issue the group was struggling with, namely, the wedge Mary had driven between God and the Church.* Mary's principle stood: "Only God knows. Canon law does not get to reality."

It can now be seen that Anne's problem with the silent couple and Mary's stand on annulment are more closely allied than it first appears. Both are concerned with the ability of the community to act in a humanly fitting way. Both have doubts about whether the community is up to it. Both suggest that the group separate itself in some way from "the Church at large," as though the group's agreements about annulment would not have to relate in any way to the Church's understanding of the matter. *Both—and here they are joined by the rest of the group—encourage the fantasy that all the group's problems exist* **outside** *of itself, either in the wider Church or in the silent couple.*

The facilitator challenged these assumptions, asking whether there were not also "hierarchies and canon laws" **within** the group itself. Some admitted this. Others denied it. The denial took a peculiar form which merits comment here. *Whenever the facilitator raised the possibility that there was fighting going on in the group, several members began to speak of the group's relation to Joe and Irene,* as though the facilitator was referring to how the group was treating **them**. This was not what he meant at all, as some members quickly caught, but no resolution of the confusion was attempted. The facilitator became anxious about whether he was being clear. However, he stuck to his conviction that *Joe and Irene and the hierarchical Church were being used by the group to deny its own inner struggles.*

In any case, no one did much about the infighting. Instead, the group tried to locate God's role in marriage. Mary continued her caution against assigning the community any role. "The growth of the couple can change the character of the community," she said. How, then, could "the community" judge when love was present? Beatrice had trouble with that. "There's not a million different loves around," she said, "there's love." Cannot the community identify it? Harry worked the hardest to find some analogy that would break Mary's dilemma. He argued that, from observation and evidence, a community can say whether an action was a cold-blooded murder or a hapless act of insanity. Why can it not say when a marriage has occurred? Mary rejected the analogy; "no set of facts can give us rather than God the right to make such a decision." This brought from Cis the comment that, "short of a vision, how can even the couple know God's decision?"

The facilitator was puzzled by these developments. *No one was adverting to Anne's painful silence.* Many, including the facilitator, were actually afraid that Anne would get up and leave the group. Secondly, the group was allowing Mary to perpetuate a confusion between divorce and annulment, despite the fact that the difference between them was already stated by the group. Why was the group avoiding the further work of explaining annulment? The facilitator thought the answer might lie in some of *the casual statements made about annulment* previously by the group. Annulment occurred in cases where things were involved like insanity, mental deficiency, concealment, bad faith, reservations, and other such negative factors. *It was a heavy picture indeed. But the group seemed to have made it in addition a nasty, terrible and dirty thing, so that* **only** *God could handle something so awful!* The facilitator prompted the group to consider this possibility, with some small success. Beatrice said frankly that, given Mary's attitude, there was no point to the discussion, since "there's no room for us." Mary thereupon relented slightly, clarifying that she was speaking of "the long run" and "the final analysis." The group produced other, less gory grounds for annulment: if a couple does not know what they are doing; if there was a previous valid marriage; if each party conceived marriage in a radically different manner; if the maturity level was so low that parties could not enter into such a contract, and so on.

This work did not last. Mary returned gradually to her view that annulment comes from God alone. She began once more to confuse annulment with divorce. *No one challenged her very vigorously* on these points, although Vic argued that, if the community can contribute so potently to a couple's well-being in marriage, it ought to be consulted in harder times. *Everyone went once around the familiar merry-go-round,* the facilitator hinting that "marriage, divorces, and annulments" might be going on in the group, *the group again taking this to refer to its relationship to Joe and Irene.* This time the facilitator challenged the group whether it was really as solicitous for the silent couple as it pretended to be. *The reaction of the group varied.* One member said, "Not terribly." Another *showed a certain amount of anger toward* (at least ostensibly) *the silent couple.* He expressed the veiled threat that the couple had better have a good reason for getting an annulment. Beatrice was puzzled at the anger. The only way it seemed to her that the silent couple's annulment could hurt the group would be to make the group "more unstable." *Beatrice seemed to have a greater tolerance for instability than some others in the group.* They were less optimistic about the community, and they showed it at this point by dragging in the (by now) tired question of whether they were supposed to be describing annulment "in this group" (as this group sees it) or "in the Church at large."

Faced with the facilitator's urging to concentrate on its own reality as a group, and to see how annulment was faring in this light, *the group continued to flounder.* Vic suggested that, since "we have a priest with us," (the facilitator) perhaps *he* could discourse on annulment. Beatrice replied marvelously, "He's a solemn member. We have more solemn members than we have anything else!" Helen admitted that annulment was such a negative topic that *she preferred not to speak directly about it;* "I don't want to talk about something that **shouldn't happen.**" Again, *the group's low view of annulment was creeping out.* But rather than face it, the group meandered around other topics. First, it speculated on what it would take to bring Irene and Joe to talk. "I thought of shaking them," said one member. Secondly, it got Harry to give a long speech about sacramental marriage, after which the facilitator remarked that there are many ways to "annul" each other in a group. Finally, it tried weakly to build on Harry's speech, but with no new insights. *Everyone seemed to be* **feeling** *now that declaring anyone's marriage to be null was an awful responsibility.* But mixed in with this feeling was the same severe moralizing about annulment that had burdened the group earlier. It was still there as the group ended.

III. THEOLOGICAL IMPLICATIONS

The marriage group manifested grave misgivings, if not scepticism, about the contribution of the community to the matter of sacramental marriage, annulment, and divorce. They just did not seem to believe that the community was that helpful. To some extent they were ascribing to a shadow-group attitudes, fears, and demands that were in fact their own. They feared making mistakes in love. They wondered how long their commitments to love would last. They linked certainty with love, and tried to cut down the risks. Or they feared not being loved by others because of a failure on their part to *be* loveable. In other words, they were perfectly normal in their approach to the topic.

Nonetheless, the group experience highlighted several aspects of sacramental marriage. First, the absence of Jesus from the discussion shows how difficult it is to bring Jesus into one's marriage in a positive way. One could only wonder whether the group really thought that his life, example, and teaching had something concrete to offer in the way of describing love. Where God hovers over the discussion, it is as the protector against unfavorable judgments by others. Marriage is, to be sure, "before God." But it is there almost as an object of his scrutiny rather than as accompanied by his concern, wisdom, support, and enjoyment. This makes it seem as though God's concern with marriage is limited to its moral propriety, but it is never quite clear to what extent the group is projecting *its own* moralizing tendencies onto God.

Second, love was seldom seen as a project, as a step-by-step affair. There was little sense that mistakes can be made in original outlays and estimates, in perspective, in planning for sunlight and shadow, in nearness to supplies and to needed information. There was no sign of the need to make provision for rerouting stubborn traits or discovering unseen faults. Rather, people's very best efforts were being measured against some all-at-once ideal from which they would inevitably fall short. Achievements in love could hardly be enjoyed; at most, congratulations for not having failed could be expected.

Yet, third, the group manifested a good sense of a couple's need to build love somewhat apart from excessive intrusion by gods and men. The trust level must be high before one can expose one's failure and hope and fear to others. This the couple learn in a tangible way from each other. And there is a blind, jumbled optimism that love *can* be found, since it has already found us.

Fourth, the community is there also, irritating by its righteous challenges, crushing by its insensitivity, helping to assess and to celebrate, noncommittal or vacillating in crisis, sharing its wisdom and its common plight, wondering about each other, praying for each other, hurting and healing as it too learns love.

Finally, the group questions whether sacramental marriage is supposed to be forever. But its concern, as we discovered, is not with this theoretical question. Its concern is with what others will do when things do not work out. So much so that, despite a few protests to the contrary, the group seems to take it for granted that love is supposed to be forever. It is the fear and distrust of others that drives the theological language into confusion (blurring the difference between annulment and divorce) and contradiction (denying that what is forever is forever). The unspoken concern of the group is about remarriage after a first marriage that was forever. There is pressure on the language to make this second marriage equally sacramental, forgetting that "foreverness" of the first marriage. But, as we suggested, this pressure is a social one more than a moral one. The morality (reality) of the situation seems to call (1) for maintaining at all costs the forever-language for the first marriage, (2) for affirming that the second marriage cannot be sacramental in the same sense, and (3) for resolving the key question of whether God and others can live with the second marriage, whether they can handle that situation or whether it must totally defeat them. And if they can, why cannot we?

VIII

The
groups
and
theology

The research in which we have been engaged was aimed at observing
how being-in-a-group influences what gets said theologically. We
presented only six actual groups. The theological areas worked on
were equally limited, although we might have noticed how sacramental questions intersect with a much broader range of theological
issues, such as Church, Christology, God-theory, pneumatology, and
so on. Notwithstanding, the base of our experimentation was narrow.
We cannot rear too large a theory upon it. In this chapter we shall first
examine in a summary way what our groups have told us about our
general theme. Then, at a further stage of generalization, we shall
examine what our groups can tell us about doing good theology.

As we begin, we should state again that what we are doing is in
many respects quite traditional. The novel aspect of it is the delib-
erate exploitation by theology of a somewhat fresh theological *locus*
(source). The task of understanding the experience of Christian faith
has always drawn from a variety of such *loci* in order to piece
together an intelligible and integrated picture of that faith. Scripture,
doctrinal traditions, Church history, philosophy, literature and the
arts, anthropology, comparative religions, psychology—in short,
the fruits of all human reflection—were assimilated into the reflection on faith that is theology.

Theology always remains what it started out to be, both reflex and
believing. The primary experience of faith carries the reflective
person along in its powerful tide. Reflex understanding of the origin,
motion, destination, dangers, and advantages of faith is really
secondary, if crucial. For this understanding the theological *loci*
provide a checklist of sorts which keeps the theologian honest, or, in

more scientific terms, keeps him comprehensive, complete, and coherent. Systematic theologians have always leaned more heavily on one or another theological *locus* to find the categories, images, and language with which to express their understanding of faith. The result is that theology gets stamped with a biblical nuance, or a literary flavor, or a historical and genetic sweep, depending on who is theologizing. By considering the group-setting as another such *locus* for discovery and understanding, a similarly distinctive stamp is given to the theology one arrives at. What we hope to show is that this contribution is not merely a matter of terminology or semantics. When considered against the background of the group-setting, important aspects of faith itself are highlighted which might otherwise be neglected.[1]

I. A SUMMARY OF THE GROUPS

If we look at our groups on sacramental theology, we can note three main preoccupations of those groups, each of which influenced the theological language which emerged.

The church

The first such preoccupation was with "the larger Church." The feelings that emerged, at least from some members, might be expressed this way: "We do not have any authority in the real world to take anything more than passive sacramental roles. We seem to be given responsibility without the ability to act. Why, then, should we bother to think theologically about the sacraments, about their precise definition, their specific contents, their benefits and disadvantages?" The influence on sacramental theology here was clearly from the shadow-group, the Church. This experience was imported by some of the members into our groups.

More precisely, the members were suffering from a certain insecurity about their roles. People have different raw talents, abilities, experiences, degrees of ingenuity, gifts, and so on. They also tend to react emotionally in highly diverse ways. Accordingly, two kinds of negotiations go on in groups. In the first kind of negotiation, a work-role is established for the individual within the group, usually in some form of job description. The group authorizes him to use his talents to work in its midst toward the common task of the group. Authorization comes from the one or ones in charge of the group, who can bespeak the group and can allow the very entry of a person into the group, as well as set limits to his role which are acceptable to others in the group. Beyond that job description, whatever work he might choose to do to further the common task, while it might be talented and resourceful, may not have the group's authorization (unless, of course, the group is previously committed to accept *carte blanche* talented contributions to the task wherever they appear).

In the second kind of negotiation, personal relationships are experimented with and tentatively established. Intimacy, sympathy, setting at ease, gaining confidence, openness, overcoming fear and prejudice, making peace with one's stereotypes—all these require much palaver, sweat, nerve, and emotional back-and-forth.

In our groups the work-role of each member was fairly well defined by the task and by the authority of the facilitator. Emotional negotiations were difficult, but that is another story. The problem we are considering here is mainly the role of the members, *not in our theology groups themselves,* but in their shadow-group, the Church. Feelings of powerlessness surround the role of many average members of that Church. Confusions exist about whether one is to perform a sacramental ministry *in* the Church (unofficially) or *for* the Church (officially). Does authorization come from Jesus? or from the hierarchy? or by virtue of baptism? from God? or from conscience? These and many other questions plagued some of the members of our groups when they considered "the Church at large."

How, then, are we to weigh these considerations? To what extent did they influence the theological work of the groups? The facilitator himself brought to the groups certain presuppositions that ran counter, in a sense, to these feelings of people about their role in the larger Church. He believed, for example, that thinking clearly about sacraments is one thing, while how to work them out in the "real world" is another. He believed, too, that the chances of ever doing anything about the real world are slimmer, if the theological language used there is poor. He believed that theological language does not merely reflect experience, but that it is a factor in changing experience. These presuppositions affected the amount of sympathy the facilitator showed to the sincere complaints in the groups about their imported problems from the Church at large. It is possible that a dynamic ensued whereby the facilitator unconsciously hampered the theological work of those members whose preoccupation was with their lack of authority in the real world. He might have *encouraged* them to wallow about in such feelings, precisely in order to reinforce his own prejudice about the irrelevancy of those feelings to the theological task. And for this he might have been "rewarded" with large doses of interpersonal fog, emotion, and sentiment by those group members.

While certainly aware of the negative image of the larger Church that some members had, the facilitator nevertheless opted to interpret their remarks about the Church as displaced or symbolic statements about *the group they were actually in* and the theological task they were actually engaged in. His reasons for doing this were these: (1) The issue of the larger Church was often introduced at points where interaction between the members of the sacrament groups was getting visibly warmer, more painful, more immediate. From that point of view, talk of the larger Church seemed like flight-language. Emotional negotiations between members of the groups were difficult. It seemed to the facilitator that people, himself included, would not fare much differently in the larger Church than they did in the groups (where they *had* authorization) precisely because of similar emotional circumstances existing in both places. So he tended to take the statements about difficulties stemming from the larger Church with a grain of salt. (2) The groups seemed almost too willing to agree with a view of sacraments in which all Christians are endowed with painful responsibility. There was no sense of *not* wanting to be authorized to do these difficult things, no candid admissions of a reluctance to "be good." *All* the villainy was deposited at the steps of the Church, a procedure which the facilitator could not accept at face value. (3) Those whose preoccupation was with the larger Church were not always concerned about their lack of authorization vis-à-vis the accepted powers in that Church. They were equally concerned about the apathy, confusion, uncooperativeness, failures, and flaws of the *general* membership. (4) The larger Church itself served, as we shall point out below, as a symbol of the way *God* runs the world. In other words, the authority of God in relationship to their own authority was at times a more real issue for the members than the authority of the larger Church.

By none of these remarks do we wish to deny that the larger Church has serious problems within its hierarchy and pastorate: with abuses of power, encroachments, self-serving silences, obfuscations and even bullying. To average laymen (and to many religious) it looks as though all decision-making power, financial control, sanctions (divine ones at that), regulatory power, and jurisdiction are in the hands of a clerical few. Moreover, their sense of powerlessness is increased by the many obligations and responsibilities they have elsewhere which render them unable even to examine the legitimacy of the status quo. Hence, they are often locked into a cycle in which only two alternatives seem recurrent and possible, total powerlessness and total power. Any voice that offers a third alternative is going to have to be convinced of this much, that the foregoing alternatives offer only a self-defeating dead end. Only with this conviction is a closer study of what really constitutes the "largeness" of the larger Church likely to succeed.

We have suggested that that "largeness" involves more than a clear and uncluttered vision of hierarchical sins. It involves a sense of being entangled with a mass of others (not necessarily clerics) whose dedication, seriousness and friendliness are either unknown or out of our control. It involves coping with our own large emotions. It involves a sea of emotional transactions with others. It involves, finally, all our preoccupations with the larger problem of God. We suggest that the groups use these complications as much as they suffer from them. When they come to theologize as a group, the shadow-group of the larger Church is a tempting convenience to enable the groups to avoid facing the here-and-now stress of interacting humanly and theologically. Only by such interaction can an adequate theology emerge. This theology in turn should address itself more in turn expressly (especially in the case of baptism, confirmation, and orders) to these specific issues of authorization, power and responsibility. And it would not be a bad thing if pastors in the Church did the same.

God and Jesus

The second preoccupation of the groups was with the kind of God and of Jesus that emerged from their own remarks about the sacraments. Though the facilitator started their reflections in these directions, this cannot explain all that happened along the way. In our groups, the fate of God in relation to the sacraments was sheer adventure. In some cases, he was totally excluded, but the silence of that exclusion spoke loudly. In other cases, God was invoked in an overwhelmingly powerful way, with no admission that such an engulfing presence makes a mockery of the modest steps which he himself supposedly encourages Christians to take in the sacraments. In still others, he was a threatening observer, a cruel taskmaster, a giant distraction, an arbitrary and edgy "inventor of new wrinkles," a competitor, a suffocating and dizzying nurturer, one who carries on secret dramas or important business with other individuals than ourselves, or one to whom we can cling with no feelings of being involved with others.

Our groups hinted at a more positive image of God, too: one who invites, who eases a situation by surrounding it with favor and promise, who neither robs us of responsibility, nor, on the other hand, measures human responsibility by divine standards, a God who is not baffled or thwarted by complexity but sustains us in the complexity of our condition.

The groups also struggled with a view of Jesus in which he loves in a vague and generalized way, with an almost maudlin and ultimately destructive affectivity, combined with a great personal dependence on a return of such affection from us. In mood and manner, the groups would have liked to anticipate Jesus' eschatological banquet. They seemed always ready for festivity, but did not seem to like to associate Jesus with work, pain, struggle, or the necessity to plod on, to begin again. The groups' Jesus cannot be specific about projects, plans, responsibilities, and priorities; he cannot base his Father's work on a clearheaded estimate of human issues. When reality dawns in the groups, a sombre quality of disappointment can be felt. "We were hoping" (Luke 24:21). Jesus is made to pay. He is now imaged as the efficient, overserious guide, steering people to correct performance (of the sacraments) whereby correct contacts (with himself, with his Father) might be established.

It matters little that sacramental activities are described in a humanly enriching way if God and Jesus remain so ambiguously in the background. Unresolved attitudes about God and Jesus influence our groups as they build their theology. These attitudes are not resolved by theology alone. But the theological enterprise presses us to integrate what we say about sacraments with a rigorously consistent view of God and of Jesus. Despite all their difficulties, our groups show us that this enterprise can advance.

One another

The third main preoccupation of our groups had to do with issues of comparative theological and emotional competence. The members of the groups rarely said to each other that one explanation of a sacrament was better than the next, or was more helpful than their own, or tied together more aspects of the sacramental experience. Basic violations of logic, fundamental confusion about the standard meanings of things, and obvious instances of saying one thing while meaning another, were rarely challenged in the groups. Or, if they were, it was in such a roundabout way that it would be hard to recognize. The result was the creation of a language environment not unlike a cluttered and unkempt street. No one was telling their neighbor to remove unsightly objects from their lawn. No one commented that some driveways were circular and well removed from the street. No one complained about the noise.

To pursue the analogy, as long as people remained simply juxtaposed, they felt safe. For, the theological exchange required at times mutual correction, disagreements, pointing out inconsistencies, and so forth. This in turn raised the issue of how the members could cope emotionally with such encounters. People are not only unsure of their intellectual and professional competence. They worry about their own emotional valence. They are even more unsure of other people on these same two levels of competence, the intellectual and emotional. In short, our groups showed that it is so possible to be exhausted by these comparative estimates that the theological task understandably suffers.

* * * * *

When viewed against the background of our groups' experience, the sacraments suffer from what we might call a certain lack of *rootedness* in the free and responsible agency of Christians. They seem, rather, a giant system of dutiful rituals, innoculations, certifications, purifications, benedictions, and dispatchings which anonymously await the individual who passes through the system. Sometimes that system is seen as the priests' thing, applied to wincing but finally grateful recipients who wander off rubbing the spot where God has touched them, puzzled by hope and proud of their passive participation. The priestly administrators are solicitous and energetic. But even with them there is not the sense of proprietory responsibility that others fantasize about them. They too are a part of the system. The sacraments they administer are someone else's—the Church's perhaps, in some disassociated and free-floating sense of that word, or Jesus', if they finally had to say who was in charge of the system. Even with Jesus, as we have seen, the sacraments are not rooted in him in a way which captures his personal responsibility and agency in their regard. Rather, they are things he sets up for us, without their ever being expressions of his sense of value, concern, and committed action in the world.

The group-experience drives us, then, to review our theology of sacraments, looking for echoes of alienation—from God, from Jesus, from each other, from ourselves—which could make the sacraments less than they might have been.

II. WHAT THE GROUPS TEACH US ABOUT DOING THEOLOGY

What we have been describing as the influence of our groups on theology is not really as negative as might first seem. For, the groups call our attention to the need for certain positive approaches, if theology is to anticipate some of the problems that people in groups have. In this section, we will explore two such positive approaches. Neither is new to theology, but the group-setting reinforces their critical importance.

Theological vagueness and the flight from responsibility
Theology must give definition and specific shape to the topics it discusses. The groups illustrated how such definition is resisted, not because people do not believe it is possible or desirable, but for other reasons. With a specific vision of Christian life, problems of responsibility, co-agency, competence, fear of failure and of success come more sharply to the fore. Factors are present which lead people to

talk about the Church in ways that equally well describe any number of benevolent associations, to speak of inspiration and revelation in terms that apply as well to all literature past and present, to confuse Jesus' incarnate status with everyman's effort to confront the human condition, to have resurrections in which nobody rises, to have good gods doing nasty things, creatures haggling with creators, everybody and nobody as priests, everything and nothing as sacrament. Those factors, as we have seen, spring in large part from our difficulties in taking roles of responsibility as our own. We live in an atmosphere of caution, in a system where issues of authorization from the group and of ultimate reprisals are unclear, and where immediate rewards are intangible. The general nervousness of people carries over into theological language. Better to keep it blurred until we all know the situation better.

Theology has to be aware of these pressures. It has to aim at greater definition rather than less, a greater refinement of its view of religious reality. It has to ask itself whether and when it has given up on the possibility of mind to catch the specificity and concreteness of reality. It cannot shy away from determining specific functions, roles, and differences. We are not suggesting here that there is a magic or arbitrary way to the "correct" definition of things in theology. Analogously to the other sciences, theology must procede by hypothesis, postulate, evidence, argument, and so on. Being limited to hypotheses is often a source of resentment and guilt for the inquiring mind, and vagueness is the sin-offering we propose to excuse our having tried to see reality. We also wish to do theology in a way that will be acceptable to all. But the groups teach us that acceptability is a poor criterion for theological work. Rather, the bond that united the groups, and that enabled them to face creatively the rugged movements of their own group-life, was precisely *the hope of a common basis for thought grounded in a shared view of some specific and definite reality.* Pain and pleasure rode with this hope. It was this hope that drew the groups forward and drew them together. Theology can express its shared view of reality in a variety of ways. But where that expression becomes so diffuse that the reality being described can no longer be identified, or can no longer be differentiated from anything else, theology is in trouble. This is less a preachment for greater objectivity in theology than it is a realization that subjectivity is more complex and demanding that we might wish it to be. It includes the pressures from the group.

* * * * *

Let us attempt a lengthy example of a theology that would pay particular attention to the concerns we have been discussing, that is, a theology that would *specify* the experience it is considering and *locate responsibilities* vis-à-vis that experience. We begin with a hypothesis which we will not have to defend immediately, but can simply state. The hypothesis is that the sick/dying person, the "candidate" for the sacrament of anointing, has a fairly definite problem. Tolstoy's instinct tells him something similar: on arriving upon his deathbed, he comments awkwardly that he does not know *what he is supposed to do*. The situation, he is convinced, has a shape. The problem of the sick/dying person, we suggest, is one of *summarizing* one's disjointed past in a favorable way. The shape of this problem can be sketched roughly, and though variations on the problem are infinite, they are variations on one and the same problem. It is a time of search, to bring a wholeness to one's personal history, to round out a picture of one's complete identity, to value it all as worthwhile. The words sound pretentious, and certainly we do not imagine that everyone would articulate in the same way this problem of summing up his or her life. Nor do we mean that an individual's life rushes before his eyes at moments of physical danger and debility. Even one event in the sick/dying person's experience may stand for "it all"—a love lost, a deed done, a house whose address is forgotten, a slight, a chance missed, a habit taken up without much notice. Any one thing can be the hinge around which all the parts move in troubled unison. The cavernous basement of Citizen Kane, with its panorama of relics from a busy and troubled life, is fed to the fires with meaningless and relentless sequence, until everything is said in one object and one memory, Rosebud.

If we can accept the hypothesis that the problem of the sick/dying person has some specific content and probable shape, we could then ask how Christians, through the sacrament of anointing, assume responsibility for dealing with that problem. Among the insightful materials in recent literature on death and dying, Kübler-Ross' description of five stages of death and dying offers an excellent framework from which to study the Christian community's responsibility toward the sick/dying person. Those stages are denial, anger, bargaining, depression, and acceptance.[2] So we will be asking how the community, at each of these stages, confronts the sick/dying person's problem of "summing up."

It is extremely hard to assume the responsibility of helping sum up another person's life favorably. It is easy to deny that this is a task to be done. It engages all our energies to consider our own past in a forgiving and benevolent way. So many faces, conversations, incidents, escapades, sheer blanks and omissions, so much trivialization, conformity, caution, viciousness, and confusion emerge in our consciousness that we are paralyzed or cowed by it all. The capacity to affirm the overall goodness of our individual past, or to see it as lovable is minimal. For, to see it thus, requires that we see it through eyes, our own or another's, that can go through it all with us and discern our lovableness concomitantly with our actual history.

It is not as though we lack experience of such behavior. Marriage and family relationships, friendships that have lasted, all illustrate the power of love to organize a person with all his detail into an acceptedness which preserves, revives, transforms, and pronounces benediction on the totality. But the strenuousness of such love taxes us even when it concerns those nearest and dearest to us. Most of us would never dare to affirm our own lovableness so unreservedly. Still less do we feel in a position to take it upon ourselves as our responsibility toward strangers.

So denial by the community begins. We hasten to provide the isolation which the sick person seeks in this first stage. He is not allowed to see the priest who will only frighten him. The community connives in shifting the sick person's problem from the here-and-now to what might happen to him in the next life. God is once more made the problem, rather than the source of our responsibility here and now. God's future judgment is substituted for our present judgment. Anointing is confused with the sick person's personal preparation for death, or even for recovery, but the community takes no more role in all of this than that of anxious observer. There is protestation that we can do nothing, except perhaps to pray. We abandon any sense of working with the sick person, with the excuse that he cannot now work. We dutifully stand sentinel at his sickness, our minds blank of any business to be done.

Or we become angry at being reminded that there is business to be done. Drawn-out suffering creates a time-frame to fill. The issue is whether it will be filled only with pain, submission, and idleness. Can we somehow fill it? We have in Scripture an excellent example of how people try to fill it, and how this effort leads to anger. The Book of Job is a classical work of theodicy, of the justification of God for allowing suffering in the world. Like a dust-covered murder file, the case of theodicy is reopened whenever evil befalls us. But the dynamics of theodicy in this case are noteworthy.

The sufferings of Job are well known. His friends try to console him. Eliphaz tries to underscore Job's former good deeds (4:1-6). But instead of continuing in this vein, he offers instead general observations on why young lions must be brought down to size (4:7-11); he recounts deep spiritual experiences of his own (4:12-21) which have highlighted for him the holiness of God. He comments on other sufferers he has known (5:1-5);he exhorts to prayer (5:8-16) and promises the rosiest of restitutions from God (5:17-27). Baldad (ch. 8) and Sophar (ch. 11) take the same tack, but nothing seems to help poor Job. In their subsequent cycles of speeches, all three consolers take a progressively angrier tone. They end up, perhaps against their wishes, saying unhelpful things like, "Can a man be profitable to God?" (22:2). Job does not seem to find solace in being told that he is a maggot, a worm (25:6), and replies sardonically, "What *help* you give to the powerless, what *strength* to the feeble arm" (26:2).

Instead, Job himself takes up the theme of his previous life's routine, covering in detail the events of his past, which he now reviews in all their discordant reality (chs. 29-31). He does what they should have done in the first place, before embarking on their pious generalizations about the plans of God. Job speaks of his tent, his children, his milk and oil, his position in town, his cheerfulness, his charities, his justice, his toughness in the service of good, his hopes, his enemies, his refusal to be vengeful, his degradation, his truthfulness, his land, his chastity, his running of his household, his alms, his attitude toward money, toward others. This is when the next interlocutor, Elihu, really gets angry. For the very detail which Job seems to be sustaining in a *productive* way poses a *challenge* to Elihu's youthful talent. No one should ask the young to sum up another's life, and that is why Elihu's speech seems so strident and unhelpful.

Jahweh, according to the story, continues the line taken by Job's "consolers." But the tradition is not clear. For, the final consolation of Job comes not through lectures, not even Jahweh's. It happens when, "all his brethren and his sisters came to him, and all his former acquaintances, and they dined with him in his house. They condoled with him and comforted him for all the evil which the Lord brought upon him" (42:11). In any case, our point in all this is to try to show how the responsibility for "condolation" can easily lead to anger, and to indicate that the optimum consolation is somehow tied to making sense of the totality of detail with which our past is strewn.

The third stage which Kübler-Ross discerns is that of bargaining. It takes magnanimity to be open to the demands of a seriously sick person, especially if they run in the direction we suggest, namely, to help them make sense of it all. There is great likelihood that concealed negotiations are taking place. Accordingly, the community might resolve to do many things in the way of its own general moral improvement rather than do that which it is called upon at the moment to do for the sick person. Provision for an attendant priest can now be resolutely made. A diffuse kindness and sensitivity can mark the community's comportment. Novenas can be said and holy pictures affixed. God can be approached with irrefutable offers. Not that these things are done with any malicious intent; not that they are not motivated by the highest kind of piety; not that they do not stem from the most poignant helplessness. It is essential to repeat that the language of consolation can be carried out in a variety of ways. But frequently enough the community is saying that it does not have the resources to help the sick person, that therefore it must "trade-off" on other assets. The suggestion here is that God may be turning the community back to the sick person with the encouragement that it *does* have the resources, if only it can bring them to bear.

Kübler-Ross' fourth stage is depression. When applied here to the community, we mean the painful realization the community comes to that consolation *is* its task. We mean the arduousness and hopelessness it experiences as it sees its responsibility as that of healing the totality of the sick person's life. There is an altruistic aspect to this depression, a strong perception that the sick person's situation seems to elude our powers to assist or to heal. There is, too, the awareness of our difficulty in assessing our own personal totality. Our flabby habits of kindness toward ourselves are now affecting our ability to help another. The task of going out of our own need to meet another's need seems too much. We count our meager resources and the inflated demands on us, and the end result is depressing.

Acceptance, which is the final stage, involves our girding for the task of consolation with determination, peace, and a curtain perspective. We will bring that harmony which we can bring. We will face the *reality* of sickness/dying in the concrete case of one person before us. What the sick person sometimes achieves for himself, we will now try to provide. Solzhenitzen's *Cancer Ward* offers us, in its main character Kostoglotov, an example of such harmony achieved:

> This autumn I learned from experience that a man can cross the threshold of death even when his body is still not dead. Your blood still circulates and your stomach digests, while you yourself have gone through the whole psychological preparation for death—and live through death itself. Everything around you, you see as if from the grave. And although you've never counted yourself a Christian, indeed the very opposite sometimes, all of a sudden you find you've forgiven all those who trespassed against you and bear no ill-will to those who persecuted you. You're simply indifferent to everyone and everything. There's nothing you'd put yourself out to change, you regret nothing. I'd even say it was a state of equilibirium, as natural as that of the trees and the stones. Now I have been taken out of it, but I'm not sure whether I should be pleased or not. It means the return of all my passions, the bad as well as the good.

The inclusion of it all in some kind of global benediction seems to be the goal. The power of the finale in Fellini's film, *Eight and a Half,* conveys this same idea. Figures and faces from a clashing past join in a circle of reconciliation and playful dance. The sense of disorder is overcome in harmony. Harmony seems possible to us only in the next life where, as Dostoevsky's Alyosha Karamazov remarks, "We shall joyfully recount all that has happened to us." In another incident, somewhere between two lives, a similar recounting is made. The dashed hopes of the living are restored by the dead: " 'Did not the Christ have to suffer thus before entering upon his glory?' And he began with Moses and all the prophets and explained to them the passages all through the Scripture that had referred to himself" (Luke 24: 18-27).

The question, then, is whether this joyful recounting can be anticipated. Do we have the capacity to urge such a vision on the sick? And what kind of God would set us such a task, or give us such a vote of confidence?

* * * * *

This brief theology of the sacrament of anointing, then, tries to embody in its language the first principle urged upon us by our experience with the groups: Give some specific content to the realities we describe or try to describe by hypothesis, and then pay special attention to how responsibilities are located around that specific content. The consolation and comfort provided by this sacrament is not something, we suggest, that is haphazard or vaguely benevolent. We have to try to pinpoint what it is that demands comforting. But to do this is to raise the question of our responsibilities more bluntly. The language of theology must anticipate the ensuing drama, speaking of the sacrament not as though it were being applied antiseptically to the sick/dying person, but rather preserving the full range of fear, hesitation, potential denial, striving, and resolve that is appropriate to the communal human situation in question.

Making metaphors

The second main approach to theology suggested by our groups is the probing of fundamental analogies, images and metaphors to such depths, with such breadth and nuance, that their use in theological explanation anticipates as many problems of understanding as possible. This principle is again a classical one. But the groups showed the disasters that occur when it is not done. Where beginnings were confused with sequels, where promises were taken for guarantees, where forgiving had no other connotation than sparing from punishment, where authority was identified with magical power and isolation, little understanding was possible for the groups.

In the general nervousness, epithet was confused with analogy. By epithet, a young boy might be called, "Smooth," "Dazzler" and

"Rotator," according to his prowess with enemy adults, girls, and sports, in that order. But epithet is understood only where terms have achieved some status of common recognition in a community. Outside of our young boy's universe, those terms would not be warranted. With epithets, however, the *assumption is* that meaning is shared. Not so with the images of theology. They mirror a more complex reality than do epithets, and we cannot always assume a shared universe of experience. Rather, we must work at unveiling our experience to each other, comparing contours, agreeing on landmarks, sharing vantage points and sightings. Another example might illustrate the necessity of this approach.

In the theology of prayer—and prayer is a dimension of all the sacraments—we are called upon in effect to work up the implication of a fundamental image. Prayer is "raising one's mind and heart" to God. The basic image is that of raising one's mind and heart to something, anything, as we might in our normal, profane experience. The "raising" has various connotations. It might convey the attitude of one bogged down in other things, and in need of separation from them. It might include an anticipation of exhilarating and uplifting sentiments. It might be a reminder of a dependent status, with stern overtones of, "and don't forget who is who here." A further sense present is of having one's attention caught, the way we are drawn to a distant noise to search out its location and possible explanation.

For some people, "mind" has useless, ultimately deceiving overtones. For others, it means curiosity, analytic tracking, overcoming doubt, stale debate, fixing on irrelevant problem solving, scanning the horizon with eyeless inquiry. It is difficult, too, to escape the nuance of "minding the store" or "minding your manners," where an element of restriction creeps in. "Heart" fares no better. It can mean desire, yearning, bursting joy; but it can also indicate flushed, constricted, heart-sick agitation. It can hint of secrets untold. It can imply candor and sincerity, an unsophisticated glance of love and contemplation toward the object or person in question. Thus, many meanings attach to the basic metaphor of "raising one's mind and heart" to something or someone.

The plot thickens when the basic metaphor is applied to prayer to God, and when prayer is described as a conversation (raising one's mind and heart) with him. Our ability to talk easily with someone usually depends on the prior expectations we have of him. If we expect a person to be solemn, we approach him accordingly. If we think he will be rational, demandingly lucid, we gird ourselves for this exchange. If we expect him to be busy or in pain or moody or dull or lecherous, titled or insignificant, we gear ourselves accordingly for the encounter. Much depends on what kind of person we think we are raising our minds and our hearts to in conversation. What expectations, then, do we have in conversation with God? How does one begin a conversation with the Almighty? the one on whom we depend for our very existence? the judge? the transcendent one? the Holy One? the Lord of history? the triune Godhead? the eternally, and independently (of us) blissful one? How does one pass time with Jesus who is judge, victim in our place, wonderful, risen, cosmic and once dead, virginal and available to so many others?

Our images could do us in unless we are careful. They could unnecessarily kill conversation. The goal of prayer is communion. It involves awareness, attention, and sometimes fixation. It is unlikely to last, or even to get off the ground, unless our image of prayer is expanded enough to include familiar entree, ready access, the expectation of work and rest, pauses, silences, disjointedness, occasional argument, some humor, mutual misquoting, rehashing and a commitment to keep going.

Images of the God of prayer, then, have to be discerned. As Rabbi Heschel said, "The issue of prayer is not prayer; the issue of prayer is God." But the theological metaphors which underpin prayer itself must also be discerned. Images that lead to charity, joy, peace, patience, benignity, and so on, are probably all right. Images which impede the fundamental task of raising our mind and hearts to God are probably suspect. Above all, we need a God who lets us move among the metaphors with a sense of freedom and ease.

* * * * *

We need, then, a theological sensitivity where images and metaphors are concerned. A theology which keeps its eye on the group, on people trying against great odds to assume a common vantage point, people stumbling against the projecting parts of each other's imagery, grasping for the whole—this theology will spend much of its time exploring the human analogies and metaphors in greater and greater detail and nuance. Only then will it be possible for a common theological language authentically to emerge.

* * * * *

III. CONCLUDING FANTASY

We have gone about as far as we can go in building our reflections about theology on the experience of the groups studied in this book. We cannot, for example, legitimately talk about professional theologians as themselves forming a group. One would think that they shared a common task, since they bear the same name and since the tradition has actually addressed them as one, as the tribe of theologians. But it is not clear that they have embraced any such common commitment. Neither are they in any immediate contact with one another, unless on a faculty, or commission or through some such arrangement. We probably should not speculate on how they might be operating, even across the contacts that *do* exist, as a group. These contacts are in fact numerous: writing, lecturing, teaching, professional associations, reviewing, journals, reading, correspondence, workshops, consultations, and so on. But we would have to consider theologians as thinking together on common themes at a great distance, and this procedure is fanciful.

If we were to pursue the fantasy, we would have to ask how the task is going. Who is on task? Who is doing other business under the name of theology and why? When do the deathly silences fall? What pairings keep the tone jaunty and confident, sweet and uncontroversial, however little this might have to do with furthering the common task? What theological segments are made to carry for the larger group (if there were such a thing) its guilt, its irrationality, its potential for violence, its agressive resentments toward the past, its exhibitionist tendencies, its fear of growing old or of becoming new? Does this process of forcing a theologian or a school to give isolated expression to these sentiments further the common theological task or not? How is competence measured? How are people quoted? Do people operate on stereotypes and fantasies? Are titles—the Catholic university theologian,the seminary theologian,the religious educator, the secular university theologian, the college theology teacher, the consultant for the bishops (or for the book companies or, indeed, for the government), the friend of so-and-so, the former student of such-and-such, the famous European theologian, the lay theologian or the woman theologian, the member of this ecumenical body or of that trend toward eastern religions—are these titles reflective of roles which feed constructively into a common task? Are they ways of avoiding the task? Do theologians build on each other's work, or do the same old false dilemmas, red herrings, gripes, and blurrings occur with disconcerting predictability? Do the theologians talk to or at each other? Where is prejudice at work and how does this influence the task of the group, if we could speak of a group? Are alliances punished and is leadership torpedoed? Does the group of theologians trust each other enough to find a common basis of experience, truth and language in its midst? Or do they settle for an exposition of all the extant theological models, when much more might be available to them? How much does the pain of the theological group—were there such a group in existence—paralyze creativity? How much does fear subvert the work of enlarging and expanding the fund of metaphor and imagery which might provide more common ties than we normally hope for? Will the group of theologians ever exclude anyone from its ranks, or is that getting too close to its own fear of being excluded? Does theology fear success? Does it beat its breast for having failed, not at its own task but at other people's? Does it measure failure by reasonable standards and moderate expectations, or does its own lack of unity as a group give rise to feelings of failure when good work is actually being done?

None of these speculations, of course, are legitimate extensions from the groups we have examined. The best we could say is that, if theologians ever did operate as a group, they might experience, along with the strenuous challenge, the dizzying fecundity and power of the group's talent to provide that kind of purified understanding of the faith that is so needed.

Notes

CHAPTER I

1 The theory and method of group analysis followed in this book derives mainly from what is called the Tavistock school. The bibliography given, following these notes, is representative of its work.
2 M. Rioch, "The Work of Wilfred R. Bion on Groups," p. 61.
3 *Ibid.,* p. 57.
4 *Love and the Person* (New York: Sheed and Ward, 1966), p. 148.
5 Sometimes a group can be doing a sub-task of a larger group having the same common purpose. In this instance, the language of shadow-group would not be appropriate for the larger group.
6 Out of the six groups described in this book, four were made up of students in a course, the other two of a more general population. Of the first four groups, two were held after classroom lectures on the subject, two before such lectures. Apart from some people finding that the facilitator "seemed different" in the course settings and outside of them, no great difference in performance surfaced in any of the six groups.
7 Other writings by the author related to sacraments are *Sacraments for Secular Man* (Denville: Dimension, 1970); *The Truce of God* (Denville: Dimension, 1972) on penance and orders, especially; *Am I Still a Catholic?* (Chicago: Claretian, 1972), and articles referred to below.
8 Sample of an observation sheet:
   In the "baptism" look for the following:
   What do the silences say?
   Does the group concentrate on the candidate's worthiness or on its own?
   Are the demands made on the candidate excessive? Why?
   Are the demands made by the group on itself excessive? Why?
   Is the group losing sight of the fact that only a beginning is at stake?

Is the group making too much or too little use of the previous lecture presentation?

How does the group use the facilitator to do or not do the task?

Do some in the group emulate the facilitator? Is this bad?

Does the group abandon its initiative in baptizing to the candidate?

When the subject of Jesus' role in baptism arises, does the group back off from its own initiative?

Does the group talk about some hypothetical baptizing group somewhere or does it talk about itself here and now?

How does the issue of infant baptism affect the group's own initiative in baptizing a candidate from its midst?

Does the male-female language affect the group in its task?

Is the group making provision for the candidate to get out of the community as it is for getting the candidate in?

Do people manifest past bad experiences with baptism?

Do individuals manifest different attitudes toward being a baptismal community, and are the attitudes frankly shared?

To the extent that they are not shared, is the progress of the baptism hindered?

How anxious are individuals that candidates for the community preserve their individuality?

What sense is there that the candidate will make a unique though limited contribution to the community?

Does the group ever beg or seem to need the candidate?

Is membership in the community being viewed as a good thing?

Do descriptions of the baptismal community tend to be doggedly rosy and nice?

What kind of God is being presupposed by the attitudes present in the group as they pursue the task?

Is the candidate interested in the kind of God being presupposed?

9 Cf. Paul Tillich, *Dynamics of Faith* (New York: Harper, 1957) ch. III, "It must always be recalled that the symbol is of value precisely as it pulls together in nondiscursive forms, propositions, desires and attitudes which discursive formulation can only brand as impossible of formulation." E.R. Goodenough, *Jewish Symbols in the Graeco-Roman Period* (New York: Pantheon, 1954) IV, 41.

10 Mircea Eliade's writings would be the most noteworthy in this trend. Hugo Rahner also had a great impact in his *Greek Myths and the Christian Mystery* (London: Burns Oates, 1963). L. Beirnaert's articles in *Eranos Jahrbuch*, 17 (1948): 255-286; 19 (1950): 41-63, are still classic. J. Danielou's work (e.g., *Bible and Liturgy*) is also representative of this trend. See also A.G. Martimort, *The Signs of New Covenant* (Collegeville: Liturgical Press, 1963).

11 E. Schillebeechx, *Christ the Sacrament of the Encounter with God* (New York: Sheed and Ward, 1963); A.M. Roguet, *Christ Acts through the Sacraments* (Collegeville: Liturgical Press, 1953); Bernard Bro, *The Spirituality of the Sacraments* (New York: Sheed and Ward, 1968); Joseph Powers, *Spirit and Sacraments* (New York: Seabury, 1973); M. Philipon, *The Sacraments in the Christian Life* (London: Sands, 1954); P. Riga, *Sign and Symbol of the Invisible God* (Notre Dame: Fides, 1971).

12 B. Cooke, *Christian Sacraments and Christian Personality* (New York: Holt, Rinehart and Winston, 1965); G. Jansen, *The Sacra-*

mental We (Milwaukee: Bruce, 1968); H. McCabe, *The New Creation* (New York: Sheed and Ward, 1964); H. Richards and P. de Rosa, *Christ Acts through the Sacraments* (Milwaukee: Bruce, 1966); J.L. Segundo, *The Sacraments Today* (Maryknoll: Orbis, 1974); A. Schmemann, *the World as Sacrament* (London: Darton, Longman and Todd, 1966).

13   B. Leeming, *Principles of Sacramental Theology* (Westminster: Newman, 1956).

14   E.g., M. Hellwig, *The Meaning of the Sacraments* (Dayton: Pflaum, 1972); C. Dillenschneider, *The Dynamic Power of our Sacraments* (New York: Herder, 1965); B. de Margerie, *The Sacraments and Social Progress* (Chicago: Franciscan Herald Press, 1974).

15   G. McCauley, "The Values of Jesus," *New Catholic World* (May-June, 1974).

16   One original meaning of the Latin, *sacramentum.*

CHAPTER II

1   N. Perrin, *The New Testament: An Introduction* (New York: Harcourt, Brace, Jovanovich, 1974) p. 279.

2   Mt. 3:13—4:22;   Mk. 1:9-16;   Lk. 3:21-51;   Jn. 1:29-35.

3   1 Cor. 6:11;   Eph. 5:26;   Heb. 10:22;   Acts 2:38;   2 Pt. 1:9.

4   2 Cor. 1:22;   Eph. 1:13;   Acts 8:16;   19:5;   Jas. 2:7.

5   1 Cor. 12:13;   2 Cor. 1:22;   Eph. 1:13; 4:30;   Acts 2:38;   19:1-6;   Jn. 3:5;   Ti. 3:5.

6   R. Bultmann, *Theology of the New Testament* (New York: Scribner, 1951) I, 139.

7   1 Cor. 12:13;   Gal. 3:27.

8   Rom. 6:2;   1 Cor. 15:29;   Col. 2:12.

CHAPTER III

1   R.B.Y. Scott, *Proverbs and Ecclesiastes* (Doubleday Anchor Bible, 1965) p. xvi.

2   *Passim* Mt. 5:25—18:28.

3   This would be more properly done in a biblical theology of confirmation, which unfortunately is beyond the scope of this study.

4   Jn. 1:33; 3:38.

5   Rom. 8:15.

6   1 Cor. 2:11.

7   Jn. 16:8-13.

CHAPTER IV

1   Mk. 2:5-12;   Lk. 5:20-24;   Mt. 9:2-8.

2   Jn. 20:22-23.

3   Rom. 4:5.

4   *Sin, Liberty and Law* (New York: Sheed and Ward, 1962) ch. 1.

5   G. McCauley, "Original Sin: What the Fighting is all About," in *The Quest for Content in Religious Education* (National Forum for Religious Educators, 1973) pp. 115-124.

6   R. Bultmann, *op. cit.,* I, 239-246.

7   See my *The Truce of God,* ch. 1.

8   *Letters and Papers from Prison.*

CHAPTER V

1 Willi Marxsen, *The Lord's Supper as a Christological Problem* (Philadelphia: Fortress, 1970); J. Jeremias, *The Eucharistic Words of Jesus* (New York: Scribner, 1964).
2 Marxsen, pp. 1-4.
3 *Ibid.*, pp. 10-11. Corroborated by 1 Cor. 10:16-17 (pp. 11-12).
4 *Ibid.*, p. 14.
5 *Ibid.*, p. 27.
6 *Ibid.*, pp. 13-14.
7 Jeremias, pp. 41-88.
8 *Ibid.*, pp. 207-218.
9 *Ibid.*, pp. 218-225.
10 *Ibid.*, pp. 225-231.
11 *Ibid.*, pp. 237-255.
12 *Ibid.*, pp. 231-237.

CHAPTER VI

1 In *The Truce of God* (ch. 4) we distinguish leadership from "official authority" on the basis of the fact that leadership is not something towards which people admit to a *moral* obligation of any sort, whereas "official authority" is.
2 This in no way detracts from the truth of the doctrine of transubstantiation which, after all, is something that *God* does when the priest, acting as the community's official, recalls the paschal mystery of Jesus.
3 In *Why Priests?* (New York: Doubleday, 1972) Hans Kung contrasts priesthood as office with priesthood as ministry. But this distinction is intellectually disappointing in the long run.
4 *The Truce of God,* ch. 4.

CHAPTER VIII

1 Cf. section III in ch. IV above.
2 *On Death and Dying* (New York: Macmillan, 1969).

Bibliography

Astrachan, B.M. "Towards a Social Systems Model of Theraputic Groups." *Social Psychiatry*, 1970, pp. 110-119.

Bennis, W., and Shephard, H. "A Theory of Group Development." In *Analysis of Groups*, edited by C. S. Gibbard, J. Hartmann and R. Mann. San Francisco: Jossey-Bass, 1974, pp. 127-153.

Bion, W.R. *Experiences in Groups*. New York: Basic Books, 1959.

Klein, E.B., and Gould, L.J. "Boundary Issues and Organizational Dynamics." *Social Psychiatry*, 1973, pp. 204-222.

Kohler, A.T., Miller, J.C., and Klein, E.B. "Some Effects of Intergroup Experience on Study Group Phenomena." *Human Relations*, 1973, pp. 293-305.

Menninger, Roy W. "The Impact of Group Relations Conferences on Organizational Growth." *International Journal of Group Psychotherapy*, 1972, pp. 415-432.

Menzies, I. *The Functioning of Social Systems as a Defense Against Anxiety*. Tavistock Pamphlet No. 3.

Miller, E.J. and Gwynne, G.V. *A Life Apart*. Philadelphia: J.B. Lippincott, 1972.

Miller, E.J. and Rice, A.K. *Systems of Organization*. London: Tavistock Publications, 1967.

Novak, J., S.J. "Theological and Catechetical Dimensions of Small Group Theory and Experience." Ph.D. dissertation. Institut Catholique (Paris), 1974.

O'Conner, G. "The Tavistock Method of Group Study." *Science and Psychoanalysis*, 1971, pp. 100-115.

Rice, A.K. *The Enterprise and Its Environment*. London: Tavistock Publications, 1963.

————. *Learning for Leadership*. London: Tavistock Publications, 1965.

————. "Individual, Group, and Inter-Group Processes." *Human Relations*, 1969, pp. 565-584.

Richardson, E. *The Teacher, The School, and the Task of Management*. London: Heinemann, 1973.

Rioch, M. "The Work of Wilfred R. Bion on Groups." *Psychiatry*, 1970, pp. 56-66.

————. "Group Relations: Rationale and Techniques." *International Journal of Group Psychotherapy*, 1970. pp. 340-355.

————. "All We Like Sheep (Isaiah 53:6): Followers and Leaders." *Psychiatry*, 1971, pp. 258-273.

Singer, D., Whiton, M.D., and Fried, M.C. "An Alternative to Traditional Mental Health Services and Consultation in Schools: A Social Systems and Group Process Approach." *Journal of School Psychology*, 1970, pp. 172-178.

Turquet, P. "Leadership, the Individual and the Group." In *Analysis of Groups*, edited by C.S. Gibbard, J. Hartmann and R. Mann. San Francisco: Jossey-Bass, 1974, pp. 349-371.

For an attempt to locate the Tavistock orientation within other schools of group-study, see Kurt Back. *Beyond Words* (New York: Russell Sage Foundation, 1972).